INDUSTRIAL ARC
of the
WEST MIDLAND
IRON DISTRICT

ASSOCIATION FOR INDUSTRIAL ARCHAEOLOGY
1991

ILLUSTRATIONS:

Front Cover: Making heavy chain cable
Title Page: The 'big swivel' c.1910
Back Cover: Forging under a steam hammer

THE INDUSTRIAL ARCHAEOLOGY of the WEST MIDLAND IRON DISTRICT
AN INTRODUCTION BY JOHN CROMPTON

Loading coal at Rowley Hall basin, Whiteheath

The West Midlands means many things to different people. This guide seeks to explain a region which depends upon economic links as they developed over the centuries, rather than one defined solely by administrative boundaries. It is a region unified by the working of iron, at first by converting and working wrought iron for the many smithing trades which supplemented the agricultural economy, and later by the phenomenal explosion of iron producing and iron manufacturing in the Black Country. 'South Staffordshire Coal and Iron District' has often been used as a synonym for the Black Country, itself a term which reached print only in 1851 and which includes parts of north Worcestershire. Lying to the north-west of Birmingham, between but excluding the old town centres of Wolverhampton, Walsall, Halesowen and Stourbridge, the Black Country is the focus and kernel of the region. In the nineteenth century the economic influence of the Black Country reached beyond its own boundaries to the surrounding towns and the countryside. This guide samples the industrial heritage of the four Black Country boroughs, the area between them and the Severn through which the first links with the outside world were formed, and a selection from Birmingham, whose success owes much to the proximity of Black Country resources.

The main physical feature of the region is a central ridge, formed by a steep anticline of Silurian limestones with later doleritic intrusions, stretching south-eastwards from Wolverhampton to

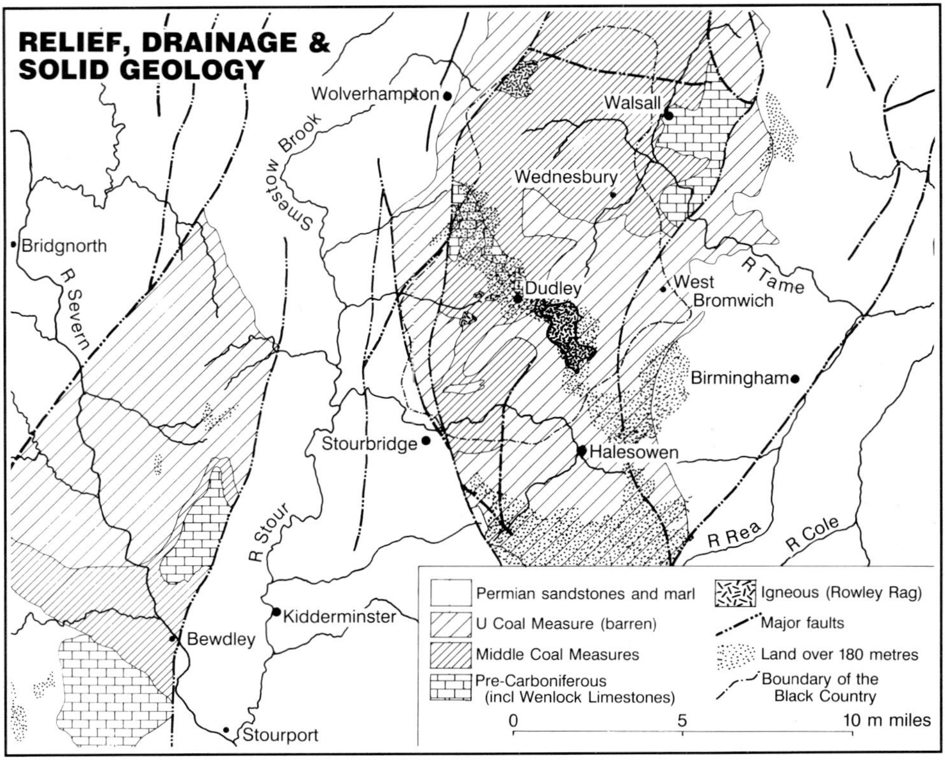

Blackheath. This ridge is the watershed of England. To the west the land surface slopes to the Severn valley, broken occasionally by scarps and ridges formed by pebble and breccia beds within the Permian and Triassic sandstones and clays, and by the tributaries of the Severn and the Stour incised in steep-sided valleys. To the east the drift-plastered upper coal measures form broad basins in the plateau, drained by the lazy headstreams of the Tame.

The seeds of industrialisation were planted early. The River Severn, a highway from the C12th, had become by the C17th a major artery for trade in iron between the scattered furnaces of the western woodlands and the water-powered forges of its steep tributaries. The Stour valley provided a natural route into the east midlands as well as potential power, and it has been said that by the late C18th it had ***on its banks a greater number of works than any stream of the same length in England***. One of the first of those works was leased in 1627 by Richard Foley of Stourbridge who, it has been claimed, introduced the slitting mill to England. Certainly he laid the foundations of a family iron business which was to last more than a century and to extend from South Wales to Cheshire. The Foleys sought to improve the supply of rod iron for smiths and nailers, as had Dud Dudley who undertook the management of his father's furnaces on Pensnett Chase and claimed later to have ***made good iron with pit-cole and made good merchantable bar***, the latter process at least being accomplished at Cradley Forge on the Stour.

Records of coal mining in the Black Country go back to the late C12th, and its ready availability helps explain the large numbers of smiths recorded in Birmingham and other towns by the C16th, already beginning the process of specialisation which later came to characterise the metal-using industries of the west midlands. This ready availability arises from the presence of the famous Staffordshire Thick Coal, the thirty-foot seam which lies close to the surface. In reality there are ten to fourteen seams, sometimes separated by thin partings and sometimes continuous, and at times the total thickness approached 50ft. With a potential yield of 300,000 tons per acre its rapid exploitation was inevitable once the markets and means of transport had been developed. In 1720

Making heavy chain cable

production was c.100,000 tons; by 1805 it had reached 1,000,000 tons and by 1864 7,000,000 tons. The traditional method of extraction was in large rectangular chambers, 'sides o' work' up to 50 yards square where the coal was removed in two layers, bottom first. The chambers were worked independently and could be closed off when spontaneous combustion of the waste slack started underground fires which burned for years. From the C19th longwall methods were introduced in the thinner, deeper seams, though there is evidence of pillar and stall working in the early C20th. By this time mining was in rapid decline, hampered by the effects of piecemeal digging, a dearth of surveys, and the lack of an overall drainage system. The South Staffordshire Mines Drainage Commission, formed in 1873, was too late to recover the situation in the Tame valley, and by the early C20th most of the eastern basin had been abandoned to flooding. The same problems had already forced the development of deep mining beyond the boundary faults, and by the 1930s the region's coal was being supplied mainly from the Cannock field to the north. Baggeridge Colliery, sunk in 1912 to the coal deep beyond the western faults, maintained a semblance of Black Country mining until its closure in 1968.

Despite the efforts of Dud Dudley around 1620, only the smithing of iron, not its smelting, could at first take advantage of the bounty of coal. There were blast furnaces in the region, and bloomeries earlier, but not until 1758 did the introduction of coke-smelting begin the region's iron revolution. John Wilkinson's furnace at Bradley soon adapted the steam engine to providing the blast, freeing iron smelting from the tyranny of water power. The new technology took a little time to grow; 6 furnaces in 1788, 14 in 1796, 55 in 1815, 123 in 1830, 200 in 1863. ***Nature did for the ironmasters all she could*** wrote Elihu Burritt in 1869, ***everything except literally building the furnaces themselves. The iron ore, coal and lime—the very lining of the furnaces—were all deposited close at hand for the operation***. Nature was not the only contributor; Wilkinson's work with Watt in adapting the steam engine to power forges and rolling mills, Jesson and Wright's 'stamping and potting' process for making wrought iron, and John Hall's pig-boiling process all helped to establish the superiority of Staffordshire 'marked bar'. With the production of iron went the manufacture of iron in all shapes and sizes; cooking pots and sad irons, plates and tubes, chains and nails, engines and bridges, axles and cart gear, locks and traps. The west midland iron district supplied the world.

Burritt saw the iron industry at its peak. The reluctance of the ironmasters to adopt new practices, and the threat of declining local supplies of coal and ore, probably did more to weaken the industry than competition from steel. The industry declined rapidly in the C20th, and only a handful of steel producers survived to become part of British Steel; Patent Shaft at Wednesbury, Round Oak at Brierley Hill, Bilston Steel Works (formerly Alfred Hickman Ltd) where the last furnace was built in 1953 and demolished in 1980. The last steel to be made in the Black Country was at F H Lloyd's in Darlaston, in 1989.

Birmingham's contribution to industry was of a different type, making up what it lacked in local resources by independence and ingenuity. The town's great asset was its freedom from the restrictions of trade guilds; indeed, only Walsall's crafts were controlled by guilds from the C15th onwards. Birmingham attracted many industries, in particular the metal trades which developed increasing specialisms and intricacies. Buttons and buckles, jewellery and guns demanded new metals, new finishes and new designs and manufacturing techniques, as they drove out the non-specialist branches, such as nail-making, to the rural fringes of Bromsgrove and Sedgley. The special trades remain, alongside the heavy engineering which has risen and begun to decline in the Tame valley to the north of the city. Transport engineering once supplied the railways with rolling stock, and now makes cars, lorries and motor components as does Wolverhampton, home of several lost causes in the history of road transport. Wolverhampton's other special industries included sheet metal work from corrugated iron through tin trunks to japan ware and enamels; and lock making, a trade it shares with Willenhall – 'Humpshire' was the name given to the district where men stooped from long hours spent filing wards and keys. Walsall is still, despite a steady decline, the capital of the saddlery, harness and fancy leather goods trades; Stourbridge still makes crystal glass; and Kidderminster is still England's major producer of carpets.

None of this development could have been effected, however, without the technologies of transport which gave this inland region its routes to and from the outside world. The Severn was an important waterway, but the development of canal engineering post-dates the early growth of the

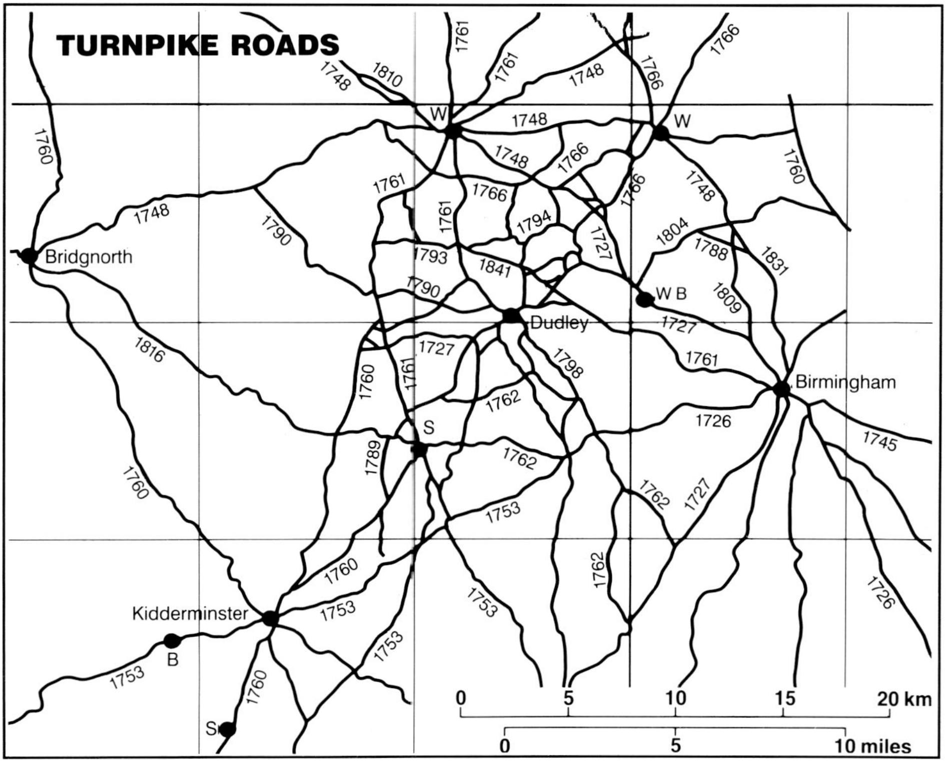

iron and coal industries. The region was bypassed by long-established land routes too, but investment in industry was parallelled by investment in road improvements. Between 1727 and 1790 a well integrated network of turnpike roads linked the towns, whilst in the Black Country coal area a very dense network developed as an antidote to the ***roads incessantly worn with the carriage of coal***. In the 1820s Telford's Holyhead Road improvements cut through the region from Birmingham towards Shifnal and Shrewsbury, and new turnpikes were being proposed and built in the Black Country until 1841.

The first elements of the region's canal system relate to the Grand Cross scheme by which England's four major rivers were to be united. The Staffordshire and Worcestershire Canal was complete from Stourport-on-Severn to Wolverhampton by 1770, and opened throughout in May 1772. By September it was joined to the Birmingham Canal, the first part of which had been carrying coal to Birmingham since 1769. Once again a dense network of branches and basins was developed in the Black Country, and direct links with the Trent (1789), the Thames (1790 and 1805), the Severn at Worcester (1815), and the Mersey (1835) followed. The Black Country canals were in constant difficulty from water shortage exacerbated by heavy traffic, and both John Smeaton and Thomas Telford were engaged to make major improvements in the 1780s and 1820s respectively. Telford's New Line through the Smethwick cutting and over the great bank through Dudley Port speaks volumes for the importance of canal carrying as well as for the vision of the engineer.

Railways played a part in bringing coal to canalside wharves as early as 1662 when Andrew Yarranton began his efforts to make the Stour navigable. The region's first steam locomotive, John Rastrick's ***Agenoria***, opened the Shut End Railway on June 2nd 1829 and hauled coal to the Staffordshire and Worcestershire Canal for thirty-five years before being preserved. But the national railway system was late penetrating the region. Wolverhampton refused the Grand Junction Railway, which was opened through the eastern parts of the Black Country in 1837 to terminate next to the northern end of the London & Birmingham, opened 1838. Whilst Birmingham became a focus of

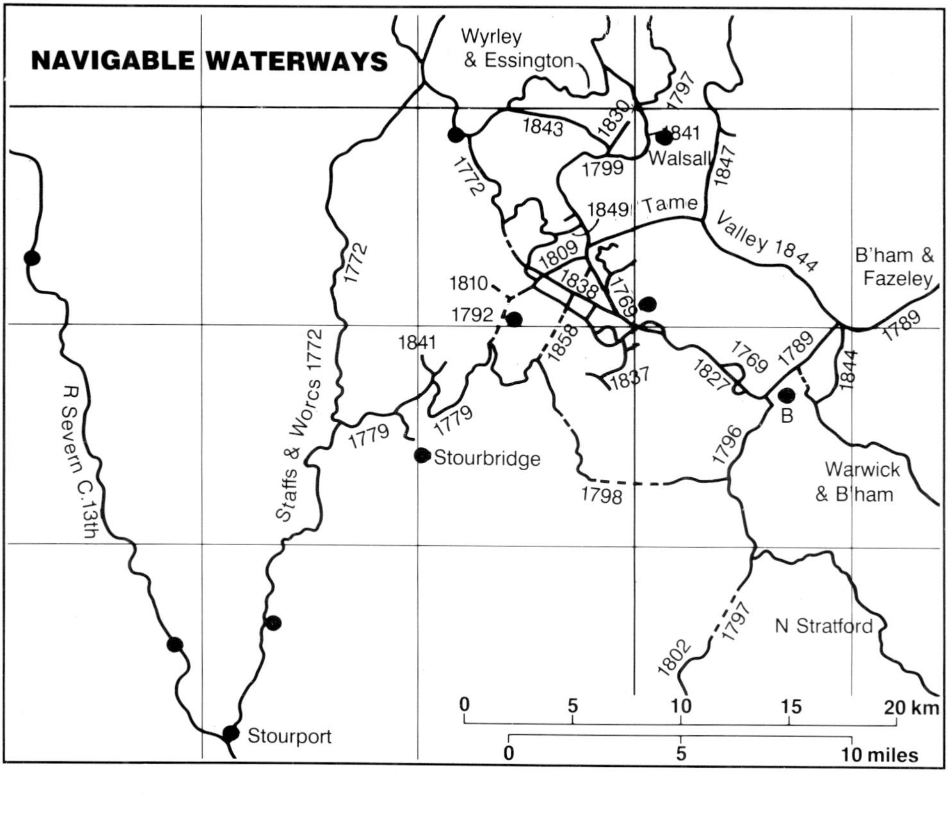

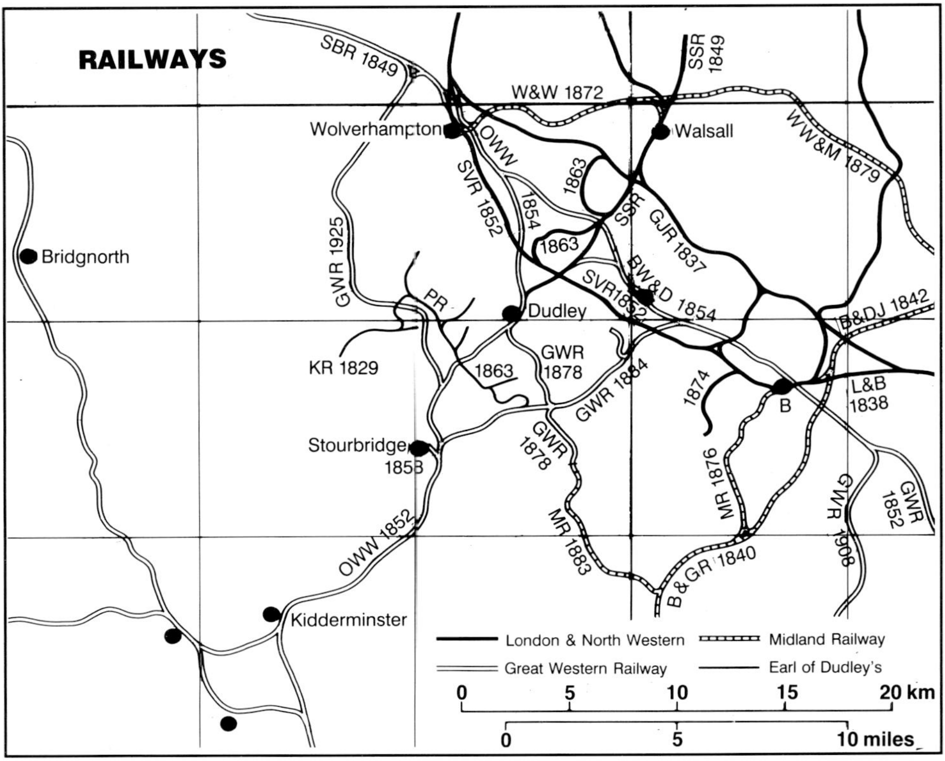

railways, the rest of the region had to wait whilst various railway battles were fought out. The Oxford, Worcester and Wolverhampton would have brought the broad gauge to the Black Country had the company not allied itself with its northern 'narrow' gauge neighbours. Instead the Great Western brought Brunel's gauge as far as Wolverhampton in 1854, and the misgivings of the Gauge Commissioners were borne out there. Amalgamations narrowed the conflict to one between the Great Western and the London & North Western, with the Midland Railway making a limited foray as far as Walsall and Wolverhampton. Again a dense network was laid down to serve the industrial areas, and the Great Western opened its Kingswinford loop as late as 1928.

The C20th has seen the decline of those characteristics, ***black by day and red by night*** which gave the Black Country, the heart of the West Midlands iron district, its name in the mid-C19th. The Black Country has changed most, because when the coalfields were drowned and the furnaces outdated, there was the greatest need to come to terms with the dereliction, the mile upon mile of ***land literally turned inside out***. Most of that land has been reclaimed during the 1960s and 70s, and covered with the kind of suburban housing estates which stifle the character of the district and make it look like everywhere else. The relics of mining are rare, the relics of iron making non-existent. Of the huge firms which built the reputation of the Black Country across the world, few remain, much reduced in size and usually in modern premises. The traditional domestic workshops of the nailers and small chain makers (a trade often followed by women) have all gone, and have all but disappeared in the lock and horse-furniture trades. Small workshops are still a characteristic of Birmingham's jewellery and gun trades, carrying out just one process and relying on the proximity of other specialists. In general Birmingham has fared better than the Black Country, for the engineering industries which established themselves at the beginning of this century in a great swathe along the valleys of the Tame and Rea have been able to adapt their production to the changing times, and the motorways have reinforced the city's centrality. The western rural areas have changed least, for the traditional industries had gone by the end of the C19th; only

Kidderminster's carpet industry managed to delay the evils of decline until the last few years. In the 1990s Birmingham is again a forward-looking city, the Black Country is no longer black, and the countryside is very green. The region is still a great user of iron and a producer of iron goods. Recession has made a resilient populace, with strong loyalties to place and a pride in their past. In the Black Country good progress is being made in the recognition and protection of industrial heritage, and this booklet hopes to encourage public and professional consciousness of the region's industrial past.

The green heart of the Black Coutry: Canal and Cobb's Engine House, Windmill End, Dudley

GAZETTEER

The gazetteer which follows is arranged in sections, dealing first with the four metropolitan boroughs which since 1974 have administered the Black Country, then with two parts of the rural west, and finally with Birmingham which deserves a volume on its own, so that coverage here is restricted to the major sites. It is intended primarily as a field guide, but some now-vanished sites have been included for their fame or place in the industrial development of the region. Information is as accurate as possible at the time of going to press, but changes are rapid and some sites may not survive. Private property should be respected.

KEY TO GAZETTEER SYMBOLS

SC	Protected as a Scheduled Ancient Monument.
LSI LSII★ LSII	Protected by Listing, as Grade I, II★, and II
CA	Conservation Area
CP	Country Park
NR	Nature Reserve
NT	Property administered by National Trust
✳	Sites which can be seen from a public place, including public streets and footpaths
❑	Sites open to the public, including public buildings, museums open at fixed hours, and canal sites where the towpaths are normally accessible to the public
■	Sites on private land or not visible/accessible
DEM	Important sites where all remains have been demolished

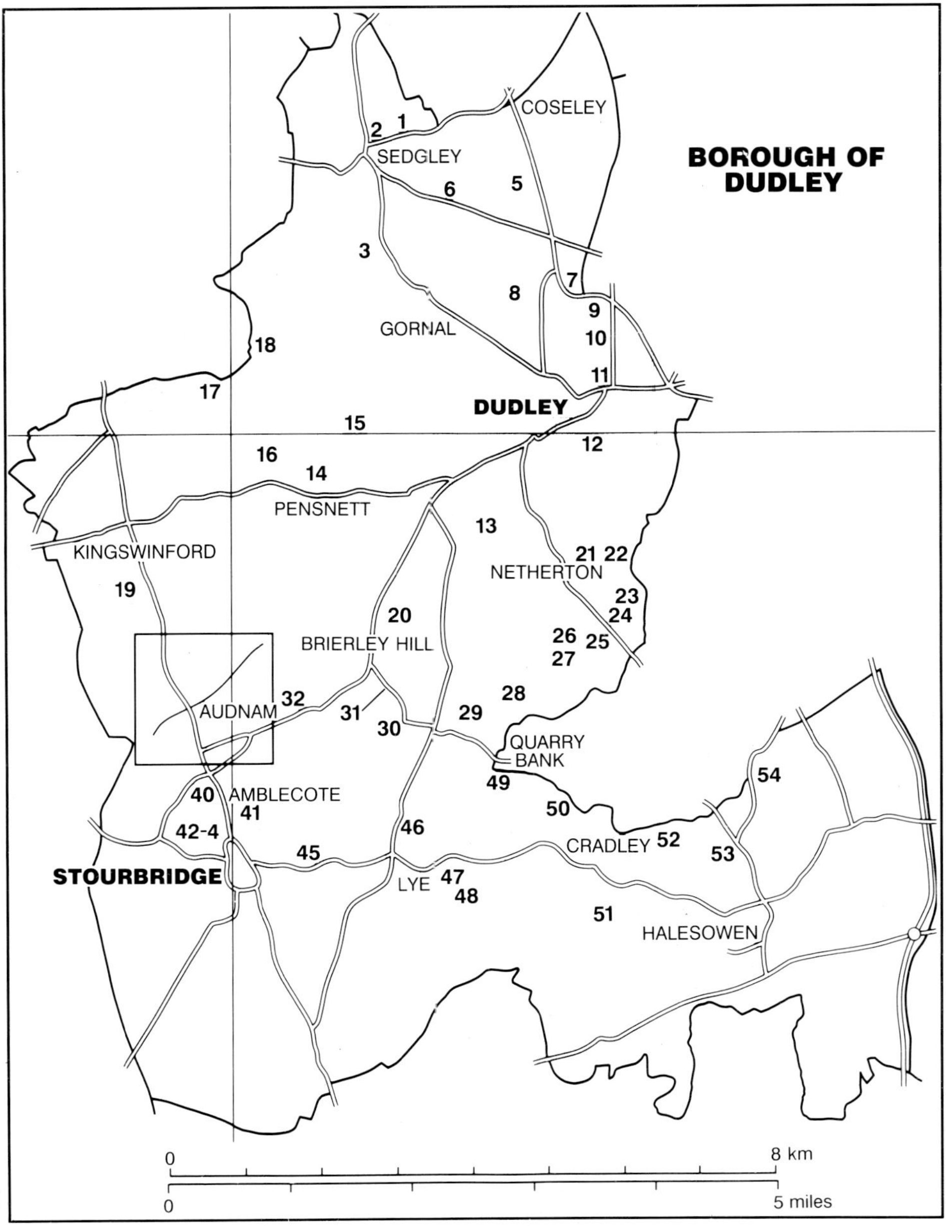
BOROUGH OF DUDLEY
COSELEY
SEDGLEY
1
2
6
5
3
7
8
9
10
GORNAL
18
17
11
DUDLEY
15
12
16
14
PENSNETT
13
KINGSWINFORD
21 22
NETHERTON
19
23
24
20
26 25
27
BRIERLEY HILL
28
32
AUDNAM
31
30
29
QUARRY BANK
49
40
AMBLECOTE
41
54
50
42-4
46
CRADLEY 52
53
45
STOURBRIDGE
LYE 47
48
51
HALESOWEN
0
8 km
0
5 miles

The metropolitan county borough of Dudley covers a much wider area than the historic borough, which was until 1974 an enclave of Worcestershire within South Staffordshire. The modern borough includes Brierley Hill, Amblecote, and parts of Sedgley and Coseley, all former Urban Districts in Staffordshire, as well as the old Boroughs of Stourbridge and Halesowen which were formerly in Worcestershire. As in other parts of the Black Country, loyalties to the old towns and villages are still strong.

The town of Dudley itself sits on a gap in the line of limestone hills separating the valleys of the Tame and the Stour. Castle Hill has been a fortress since the early eleventh century, though the present castle is C14th and later; the Tudor extensions were the home of the Earls of Dudley until 1750, and were incorporated in Dudley Zoo in 1937. The town retains its wide medieval High Street, but most development came in the 18th and 19th centuries with the growth of industry in the Black Country. The American Consul in Birmingham described the view from the castle at night, *a scene unparalleled on the globe—a thousand furnaces white at the mouth, setting the clouds on fire* (1869). The hilltop town remained free from the ravages of the mines and furnaces which surrounded it, though it could not have escaped the smoke and dirt; in 1852 the Board of Health's inspector wrote *in no other part of England .. is the work of human extermination effected in so short a time as in the district surrounding Dudley*.

The modern borough embraces parts of the upland spine and much of the western basin of the Black Country. Despite the inexorable spread of suburban estates there are still islands of green where small farms rubbed shoulders with industry. The relics of mining have largely disappeared, except where the steeply dipping Wenlock limestones were followed from surface chasms to underground caverns pierced by navigable canal levels. Iron furnace slag is more enduring, and often provides sites for modern industrial sheds or, as at Round Oak, Britain's second largest out-of-town shopping complex. The industries of the Stour valley continue to decline, and the traditional industrial buildings of the area, the chain and nail shops especially, are becoming rare. Yet there are some notable examples of conservation in the borough: the late-eighteenth century industrial hamlet at Mushroom Green with its chainshop; the work of the canal societies at Stourbridge and in the Dudley Tunnel; the Black Country Museum which was initiated and has been generously supported by Dudley Borough Council. More recently the Planning Department has commissioned studies of the history and building stock of the industrial period, an example to be encouraged elsewhere.

DU1 THE BEACON BREWERY

Bilston Street, Sedgley.

SO 923940 ❑

A small tower brewery behind the Beacon Inn, a finely-maintained example of a typical Black Country pub. The brewery was out of use from 1956 to 1987, when it once again began to brew 'Sarah Hughes Dark Ruby Mild'.

DU2 COTTAGE BLINDS

Brick Street, Sedgley.

SO 918939 **LSII** ✻

A stone building with arched cast windows, this former nail warehouse dates from the early C19th and testifies to the important outworker trade of nail-making in the district.

DU3 RUITON WINDMILL

Vale Street, Upper Gornal.

SO 919924 **LSII**

The small tower built of local stone and dating from c.1820 survives, with the adjacent miller's house.

DU4 COSELEY CANAL TUNNEL

Ivyhouse Lane, Coseley

SO 941941 ✻

Brindley's Birmingham Canal took a sinuous contour course through Bradley and Wednesbury Oak. Telford's 1824 survey recommended a deep cutting through Coseley Hill, but the 360yd tunnel with its two towpaths was not completed until 1837, shortening the Birming-

Limestone Mines, Castle Hill, Dudley

ham Canal by more than three miles. Ivyhouse Lane passes over the north portal, and provides a view of the wide approach cutting.

DU5 COSELEY WINDMILL

Oak Street, Roseville.

SO 938933 ✱

A small 3-storey whitewashed brick tower, now converted as a dwelling with modern attached house.

DU6 TURNPIKE ROAD

Sedgley to Tividale.

SO 950936 to 973907 ❑

Included because of the late date of its enabling Act in July 1841, the road bypassed Dudley. Impressive embankment at SO 933921. The c.1844 tollhouse from Littleworth (SO 937927) was moved to the Black Country Museum in 1989.

DU7 BIRMINGHAM NEW ROAD

Coseley to Burnt Tree.

SO 936944 to 962904 ❑

First proposed in 1908, but not constructed until 1924-27 as a three-lane road with government aid for unemployment relief (SA45). It cut across mainly derelict land with no concern for existing road patterns.

DU8 WRENS NEST LIMESTONE MINES

off Hillside Road, Dudley.

SO 936919 NR ❑

The Wrens Nest is one of the hills formed where a sharp anticline brings Wenlock limestones to the surface. They were an important source of lime for building and agriculture, but were especially exploited for the iron industry. Gaping holes (fenced) lead down to underground caverns at and below canal level. At SO 935918 a cottage and the remains of two horseshoe kilns survive at the site of the Wrens Nest Lime Works. Abraham Darby was born at Wrens Nest, his father being a farmer and locksmith.

DU9 DUDLEY CANAL TUNNEL

off New Road, Dudley.

SO 947917 ❑

The eastern section is Lord Ward's Tunnel, 196 yards long and opened in 1778 to provide navigable access to underground limestone mines. In Castle Mill Basin, once subterranean, are the entrances to the main tunnel, 2942 yards long and completed 1792, and the now blocked Wren's Nest tunnel, 1227 yards long and cut 1805-37. The Dudley Canal Trust operates boats into underground mine chambers through new tunnels, completed 1984 and 1989 (admission charge).

DU10 THE BLACK COUNTRY MUSEUM

Tipton Road, Dudley.

SO 949914 ❑

A 26-acre site established in 1976 where local buildings are being rescued and reconstructed to recreate the characteristic landscapes and life of the Black Country in the early C20th. Includes a hand-fed iron rolling mill, anchor forge, chain, nail and glass engraving workshops, canals with a boat-dock, operating tram and trolley buses, pub, chapel, houses, shops, coal mines with a replica 1850s drift, and a full-size working replica of Newcomen's 1712 engine, the original of which was very close to this site (admission charge).

DU11 RAILWAY GOODS SHED

off Castle Hill, Dudley.

SO 949908 ✱

Long wooden goods shed formerly with access through four side doors with awnings. Pre-1884, but vertical boarding with weatherstrips suggest an earlier date. The Oxford, Worcester & Wolverhampton Railway reached Dudley in late 1852, was closed in 1962 and the station has been demolished.

DU10 The Black Country Museum: *left*, Limekilns and the canal from the re-erected Broad Street Bridge and *below*, the Dudley Stourbridge tram

DU12 BEAN CAR FACTORY
Hall Street, Dudley.
SO 947900 *
The company of A Harper Sons and Bean had its origins in the 1820s as makers of fenders and fireirons. During the First war a large munitions factory, the National Projectile Factory, was built at Hall Street. From c.1920 cars were made, and from 1925 car bodies were fitted to chassis' driven from the Tipton Green assembly plant (SA4). The 1925 offices, with a prominent scroll over the door announcing 'Bean Cars', are currently empty.

DU13 CANAL LOCKS, TUNNEL PORTAL
Parkhead, Dudley
SO 933890 ❑
The Dudley Canal (1779) rises through Blowers Green Lock (which itself replaced two locks in 1894) above which three locks rise under a GWR railway viaduct to the south portal of the Dudley Tunnel (2942yds, 1792). Branch canals each side of the top lock, now filled, served local ironworks. At SO 936897, behind the library, is a 'pepper pot' tunnel ventilation shaft. The late C19th pumping station at Blowers Green lifted water to the tunnel (453ft) level.

DU14 BARROW HILL RAILWAY INCLINE
Tansey Green.
SO 911900 to 913892 ❑
A rope-worked incline on the Earl of Dudley's Pensnett Railway built c.1856 to connect the railways of Pensnett Chase with those of the Round Oak Iron Works. Despite the gradient of 1 in 25 it was later worked by locomotives, and there was a locomotive shed at SO 909903. At the foot of the incline branches served brickworks and coal mines on both sides of the railway, and vestigial spoil tips can be seen. The railway closed in 1966.

DU15 ENGINE BED AND CHIMNEY
off Hunts Mill Lane, Gornalwood
SO 915902 *
A 40ft brick chimney with diaper pattern in yellow and blue brick, and a blue brick engine foundation in the middle of a field mark the site of Old Park Colliery's Pit 60, later Himley Colliery Pit 12, sunk c.1870 and disused by 1938.

DU16 TILE WORKS
Dreadnought Road, Pensnett
SO 905896 *
The 'Dreadnought Works' of Hinton Perry & Davenhill which made a variety of brick and terracotta as well as the famed roofing tiles, from c.1805. Known as 'no manses' because most of its 300 workers were women.

DU17 OAK FARM BRICKWORKS
Ham Lane, Kingswinford
SO 897905 *
William Mobberley's works (formerly John Walker's) has made firebricks since 1860. Some 'beehive' downdraught kilns are still in use in early 1991, and there is an old hand-operated wire-cut machine and an early tempering tub and pugmill. Hand moulding by women is a long tradition, and one woman still works here. Recorded on video by IA Recordings. Visitors are not welcome.

DU18 TOLLHOUSE
Himley Road, Gornalwood
SO 903911 *
A tiny toll cottage guarding the junction of Brickkiln Lane and Himley Road, the latter turnpiked 1790. Close by are traces of the pools which powered Dud Dudley's Hascoe Wood furnace.

DU19 BROADFIELD HOUSE GLASS MUSEUM
Kingswinford
SO 898881 ❑
A former Georgian town house houses a museum featuring the products and methods of the local decorative glass industry.

DU20 (site of) **ROUND OAK STEEL WORKS**
Dudley Road, Brierley Hill
SO 922876 **DEM** *
The Level New furnaces formerly leased by the Earl of Dudley, were rebuilt and taken under direct control in 1846-7. In 1856-57 a modern ironworks was planned and built, with 54 puddling furnaces by 1873, and its products achieved a high reputation. Steel was first made in 1890; the Earl of Dudley's Round Oak Steel Works became part of British Steel in 1951, and closed in 1986.

DU21 GALLOWS CRANE
St Peter's Road, Dudley
SO 950883 **SC** *
A rare timber gallows crane still stands on what was a wharf in the former Harris's boatyard, which operated until 1960. The adjacent miniature tower windmill is a poor pastiche.

DU22 NETHERTON CANAL TUNNEL
Windmill End, Dudley
SO 953883
The last classic canal tunnel built in Britain, it was completed in 1858 in the grand manner with 17ft waterway and two towpaths, lit first by gas and later by electricity (SA43). The portal is an early example of the use of Blue Staffordshire engineering brick. The canal approaches on a sinuous contemporary embankment; the original alignment was similar, but continuous

DU21 Gallows Crane, Bumblehole, Netherton

subsidence forced the Dudley Canal Company to build the Bumblehole contour loop, parts of which survive. At the junction of the Dudley No 2 line to Halesowen are four fine cast roving bridges, one marked 'Toll End Works' (near Great Bridge).

DU23 WITHYMOOR FORGE
Northfield Road, Netherton
SO 950877 ✻
Established 1780 by James Griffin, with water-driven hammers making scythes. The site is now J T Parkes with a late C19th office, whose ground floor cast windows show how it has subsided relative to the adjacent canal, fronting modern buildings. Across the road at Samuel Lewis's, makers of a vast range of small agricultural tools and harness chains since c.1760, is a single storey workshop with the traditional unglazed barred windows.

DU28 Mushroom Green chainshop

DU24 WITHYMOOR INTERCHANGE BASIN
Halesowen Road, Netherton
SO 949876 ✻
A series of canal wharves served by a short railway branch from the former Blowers Green to Old Hill (GWR) line, and designed for interchange of traffic between rail and canal. Part overgrown, part used as moorings.

DU25 (site of) **NOAH HINGLEY & SONS LTD**
Netherton
SO 948875 **DEM** ✻
In the nineteenth century Hingleys was a huge self-sufficient empire with its own coal and iron mines, blast furnaces, puddling furnaces and rolling mills, chainshops and anchor works. The Black Country's first chain cable was made here in 1820, and its first anchors in 1838. The works were gradually run down and the site cleared for new factory units in 1989.

DU26 LLOYDS BRITISH TEST HOUSE
Primrose Hill, Netherton
SO 944874 ✻
This was the last of many chain test houses operating in the district, testing very large chain and anchors; the *Titanic* bow anchor was assembled and tested here. The long building by the Dudley Canal, much altered, closed in March 1990.

DU27 PRIMROSE BANK CANAL WHARF
Cradley Road, Netherton
SO 945873 ✻
The canal towpath passes over a large bridge giving access to a small canal basin established by the Shropshire Union Railway & Canal Co. The wooden warehouse, now minus its awning, clearly demonstrates its LNWR origins; 'London Midland & Scottish Railway' was legible on a long wooden stable block until its demolition in 1989. The whole site is built on the hillside, supported on brick and concrete retaining walls.

DU28 MUSHROOM GREEN HAMLET
off Quarry Road, Dudley Wood
SO 937866 **CA** ❑
The best remaining example in the Black Country of a settlement formed by the leasing of haphazard plots from the Dudley estates for building, and now containing examples of workers' cottages from the late eighteenth century to 1977. Originally a settlement of miners and nailmakers, the latter were forced by the introduction of machine-made nails c.1830 to adapt their skills to chainmaking. In 1835 John Griffiths established himself as a handmade chain maker and dealer for workshops in the hamlet. The family emigrated to

Australia in 1912, but the firm continues as Griff Chains Ltd in new buildings, though in 1991 their electrically welded chain making was transferred to Foxoak Street, Cradley Heath (SA52), and chainmaking at Mushroom Green ceased. The family house still serves as offices, and part of the old works, with wheels still set in the wall for passing chain out to waiting carts, was refurbished as garages in 1977. A six-hearth chainshop (**LSII**) is preserved as an outpost of the Black Country Museum, and demonstrations are given on the first Sunday of each month in summer.

DU29 NOAH BLOOMER & SONS
Oak Street, Quarry Bank
SO 929862 ✻
Established in 1850, the last large company to make hand-made chain, up to the winter of 1976. The present buildings housed the manufacture of open link and cable chain up to 1•5 inches (the diameter of the rod used, not of the finished link). The company is still in business supplying chain.

DU30 DANIEL BATHAM'S BREWERY
Delph Road, Brierley Hill
SO 922864 ❑
The Bull and Bladder with its Shakespearian quotations fronts the plot, and small tower brewery to the side and behind. One good reason for the fame of Black Country beer.

DU31 DELPH NINE LOCKS
near Mill Street, Brierley Hill
SO 920866 ❑
Despite the name there are now only eight locks. The original lock flight of 1779 incorporated two- and three-lock staircases, but following mining subsidence the middle seven were replaced in 1858 by six separate locks on a new straight alignment. Fragments of the original line can be seen to the east of the present alignment, and an octagonal-gabled keeper's cottage dating from c.1779 (BCN 151) survives. A late C19th stable block has been restored as an information centre.

DU34 Dock Stores tommy shop, Audnam

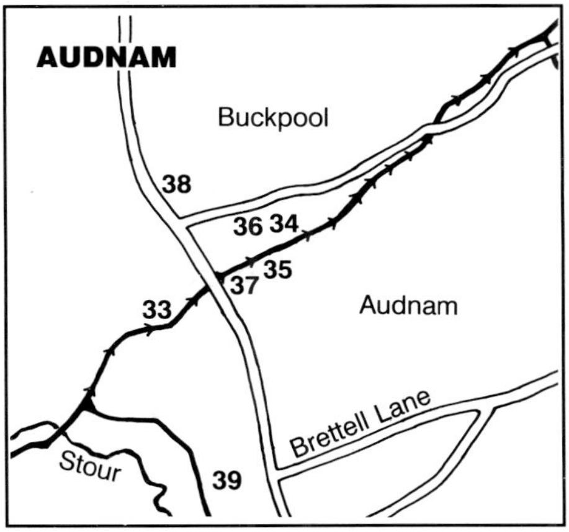

DU32 HARRIS & PEARSON BRICKWORKS
Brettell Lane, Brierley Hill
SO 907864 ✻
The Company established this 'Newside Works' in 1872, constructing an elaborately decorated office and weighbridge as an advertisement for their own firebrick and buff terracotta products. Firebrick and large refractory blocks for the local glass industry are still made.

DU33 WORDSLEY LOCKS
Stourbridge Canal, Audnam
SO 890863 to 903872 ✻
The Stourbridge Canal rises through a flight of sixteen locks from the Stour valley to Pensnett Chase. Completed in 1779, the locks present an attractive landscape of subsidence and repair, with many associated features (D34, 35, 37). At SO 927867 two locks are only a few feet apart as at The Bratch (SS2), with a centrally split iron tail bridge and an early C19th lock cottage.

DU34 DOCK STORES AND OFF-LICENCE
Oak Road, Audnam
SO 897867 LSII ❑
An interesting cluster of buildings pre-1840 (when it included a smithy and stables), adjacent to Locks 9 and 10 of the Wordsley flight. The shop is thought to have been a 'tommy' shop.

DU35 DADFORD'S SHED
Mill Street, Audnam
SO 895866 ✻
A wooden canal warehouse built c.1890 on the 'island' between Lock 12 of the Wordsley flight and its pound. Open to the pound with an awning. Originally a transit shed for seeds and hops destined for Webbs nearby (DU36), it has since seen various uses.

DU37 Glass engraving department, Staurt Crystal, c1905

DU36 FLOUR MILLS WAREHOUSE
Mill Street, Audnam
SO 895867 ✻
An imposing five-floored warehouse of dark red brick, built 1895 by Webbs, who were well-established seed merchants and maltsters.

DU37 STUART CRYSTAL GLASS WORKS
High Street, Wordsley
SO 894864 **LSII** ❑
Red House glass cone is the only complete cone surviving in the area, and one of only four surviving in Britain. It was built c.1780 and has been restored in recent years as part of a visitor centre, with air flues excavated, a modern central glass furnace, and a preserved annealing oven. Adjacent buildings exhibit some of the company's history and procucts and there is a factory shop.

DU38 ART AND TECHNICAL INSTITUTE
High Street, Wordsley
SO 892868 ✻
Built in two phases, 1897 and 1907, in highly decorated Art Deco style with finely modelled terracotta panels, and intended to teach and encourage artistic development for the enhancement of the local glass trade. It is threatened by a road widening scheme and there are plans to reconstruct it at Stuart Crystal (D37).

DU39 PLATTS GLASS CONE
off Platts Road, Audnam
SO 893858 ✻
The remains of a glass cone stand about 14ft (4m) high. Best seen from the canal towpath. The company was established in 1838.

DU40 'THE FISH' TRAM DEPOT
Wollaston Road, Amblecote
SO 897855 ✻
The Kinver Light Railway opened from here in 1901, and a battery booster station was provided in 1902. A new four-road car shed with waiting room and electricity sub-station was built in 1905, and three more roads were added in 1908 and 1914. The depot closed in 1930, but the parcels office and waiting room are now a sub-station and the shed still contains two tracks.

DU41 PARISH CHURCH
High Street, Amblecote
SO 900850 ❑
Designed by Samuel Hemmin and completed 1842, built of yellow firebrick made at J W King's Withymoor Works. Most of the cost was donated by the ironmaster James Foster.

DU42 THE BONDED WAREHOUSE
Canal Street, Stourbridge
SO 899848 **LSII** ❑
Built 1799 as a single-storey 'bond' for the storage of wines and spirits close to the terminus of the Stourbridge Arm, it was extended later to three storeys. Brick-built with the canalside elevation supported on cast columns and a curved east gable, it has been restored by the Stourbridge Navigation Trust for exhibitions and meetings. The offices of the Stourbridge Canal Company survive on the south side of Canal Street.

DU43 WHARF AND DRY DOCK
Stourbridge Canal
SO 894849 ✻
Close to the sharp bend to the terminal basin, Bradley's Wharf and the adjacent dock were excavated in 1988 to reveal fragments of rail lines and a crane base. At the bend a towpath bridge cast at Coalbrookdale spans a canal arm once leading into Bradley's works. Bradley's manager's house stands derelict behind the site.

DU44 THE NEW FOUNDRY
Bradley Road, Stourbridge
SO 894848 **LSII** ✻
A famous ironworks established 1800 by John Bradley, later joined by James Foster and from 1819-1831 by John Rastrick. Famed for many cast and rolled products including much of the fishbelly rail for the Liverpool & Manchester Railway, and Rastrick's locomotives *Agenoria* of 1828 and *Stourbridge Lion*, one of three exported to America in 1829. The 'New Foundry' designed by Rastrick and built in 1820 featuring a spectacular iron roof with wrought iron rafters and cast iron tie bars, has remained in continuous use.

DU45 STAMBERMILL VIADUCT
Birmingham Street, Stourbridge
SO 910843 *
The Oxford, Worcester and Wolverhampton Railway (1852) crossed the Stour valley on a wooden trestle viaduct of Brunelian character, replaced in 1882 by ten brick arches on the west side. The abutments and one brick pier of the original trestle remain.

DU46 STEAM HAMMER
Dudley Road, Lye
SO 924849 ❑
A brightly painted steam hammer, made by Davy United, forms a monument at the entrance to Lye Forge, now an industrial estate.

DU47 BAKER'S HORSESHOE WORKS
36-37 King Street, Lye
SO 926841 *
The company was established to make frost nails (to prevent horses slipping on ice) c.1890, and still makes a large range of horseshoes. The works is fronted by late C19th buildings which were designed to be easily converted to cottages in the event of business failure.

DU48 SPRINGFIELD WORKS
Careless Green Road, Lye
SO 927839 *
A complex of 2-storey brick workshops with cast iron windows, curved to fit an irregular site between three streets. It was built c.1890 for John and Daniel Croft, Galvanisers and is now a tool grinding works. The manufacture of sheet metal buckets, baths etc, which were then galvanised was carried on in many small workshops in the surrounding area, and a mixture of houses and industrial buildings makes this a fascinating area.

DU49 (site of) **CRADLEY FORGE**
off Forge Lane, Cradley
SO 934856 *
Dud Dudley claimed to have smelted iron with coke c.1618, and in his *Metallum Martis* of 1665, he claimed to have wrought his iron at a forge called Cradley. There was certainly a furnace by 1610, and its foundations on the south side of the Stour were reported in 1912. The site has been cleared and part built over, but brickwork can be seen in the river bed. The Mousesweet Brook enters from the north bank, where there are fragments of ironworks buildings in the steep bank, and the footings of a bridge which carried a turnpike road until it was diverted for the building of the railway in 1863.

DU50 CHAINSHOP
Butchers Lane, Cradley
SO 943852 *
A brick-built four hearth chainshop operated by the Nock family for 150 years until 1941-42. When recorded in 1973 it still contained the remains of 'tommy' hammers and bellows buried under mounds of firewood.

DU51 LUTLEY MILL
Lutley Lane, Halesowen
SO 949837 **LSII** *
An early C19th 4-storey brick building on site of an earlier mill, built into a steep bank, it was converted for residential use c.1974, retaining some original windows and sack doors.

DU52 NEW HAWNE COLLIERY
Hayseech Road, Halesowen
SO 957846 **LSII** *
The last significant surviving colliery site in the Black Country, New Hawne was sunk 762ft. to the Thick Coal in 1862-65, worked by the New British Iron Co as part of the Corngreaves estate until 1895, and closed in 1926. A winding house, a rare example of a Guibal fan house, and a long range with smithy and offices survive, but unloved.

DU53 (site of) **HALESOWEN FURNACE**
Furnace Hill, Halesowen
SO 966846 *
A charcoal furnace operated from 1602 to 1772, after which the site became a slitting and rolling mill and later an anvil, vice and spade forge. It continued as a spade and shovel forge until c.1920, and some minor buildings may relate to this. There is no trace of the furnace, but a heavily-built weir immediately downstream of the road bridge can be seen. An early C18th. tramway from Haden Hill Colliery to the Dudley Canal passed close to the site crossing the Stour by an impressive stone and brick bridge.

DU54 COOMBESWOOD TUBE WORKS
off Coombes Road, Halesowen
SO 971855 *
Established in 1805 by Abraham Barnsley; bought by Lloyd & Lloyd in 1870 and extended, it became Stewarts & Lloyds in 1953. Tubes were transported in the works by canal boat until the late 1970s. The south end of Gorsty Hill Tunnel (Dudley No 2 Canal) is inside the large site, only part of which is now used.

DU52 New Hawne Colliery Buildings

DU33, 35 & 37 Canal, Dadford's Shed and Stuart Crystal glass cone

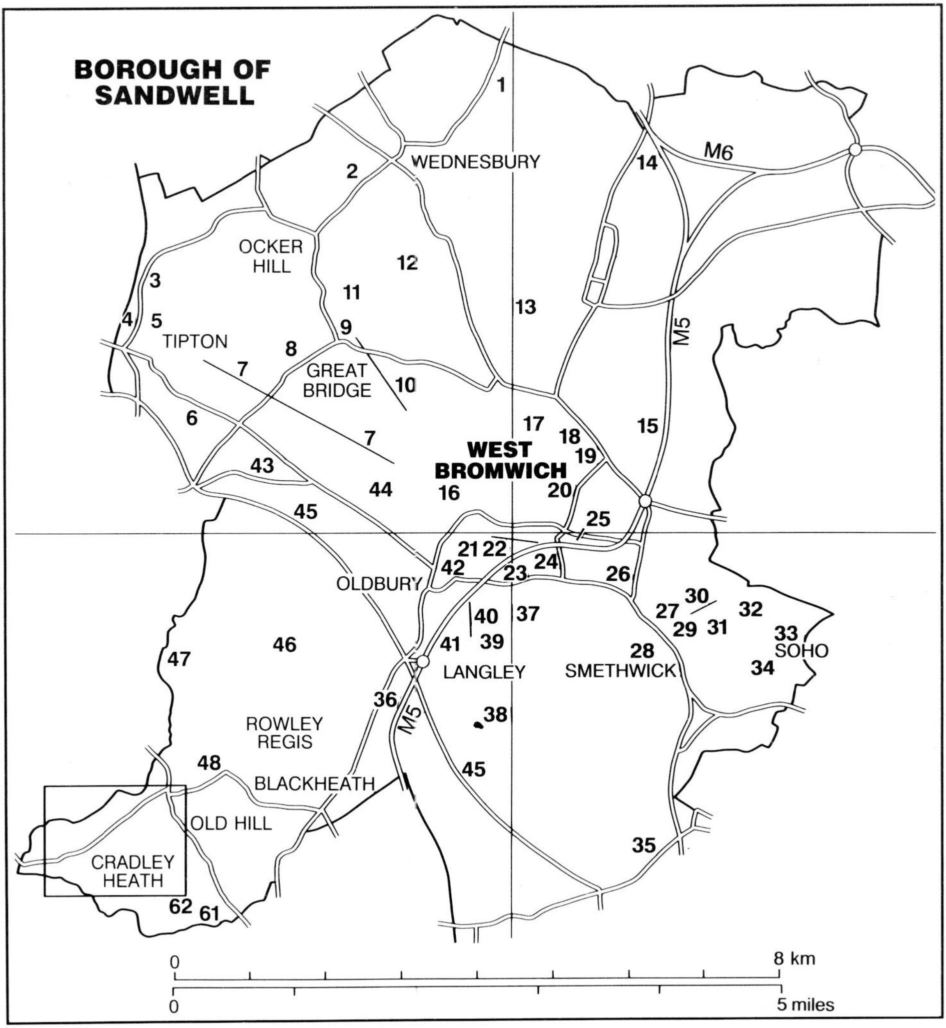

BOROUGH OF SANDWELL

The Borough of Sandwell is the least comfortable of the metropolitan boroughs created in 1974. The post-war planning report 'Conurbation' identified the fragmentation of local government control as one of the elements contributing to the decline of the Black Country economy, and the Borough of Sandwell brought together the previously separate urban districts of Wednesbury, West Bromwich, Smethwick, Oldbury, Coseley (part), Tipton and Rowley Regis. The result is a disparate borough with boundaries which are definitely not represented in the landscape, taking in much of the eastern coal basins but straddling the upland ridge to include Old Hill and Cradley Heath in the Stour Basin. In an area once described as straggling villages interspersed with waste heaps, loyalties to place are still paramount.

Lying on the Holyhead Road, West Bromwich has been the dominant town, with a long-established range of metal-using industries from foundry work through cart-gear and springs to glass. Open land to the south of the town and close to the lines of canal provided the locations of large concerns, such as the Metropolitan Carriage and Wagon Works, Salters Springs and Avery's who took over the site of Boulton & Watt's Soho Foundry established in 1798. Chance's Glass Works, whose major fame was to produce the glass for the Crystal Palace, straddled the canal between West Bromwich and Smethwick. Nearby Oldbury had its boiler works, chemical works and the Oldbury Carriage and Waggon Company. Close to the valley of the Tame, where the Staffordshire thick coal was mined so haphazardly as to outrun any capacity to remove water, the tube drawing and structural ironwork industries congregated, together with the large ironworks which lined the canals into Great Bridge, Tipton and Coseley. West of the Rough Hills, which are still disappearing under the onslaught of quarrying the 'Rowley Rag', Sandwell's sector of the Stour basin is the undisputed capital of chain-making; in 1928 90% of Britain's chain was made here.

Whilst Sandwell's turn-of-the-century housing stock has been the target of much demolition, there have been some notable heritage successes, in particular with the Galton Valley corridor through Smethwick where some notable canal sites are being safeguarded. Considerable areas of the Borough lie within the sphere of the Black Country Development Corporation, which has sponsored the publication of RCHM(E)'s Record of the designated area's building stock.

SA2 Old Park Works, Patent Shaft and Axletree Company

SA1 WOOD GREEN WATERWORKS
Brunswick Road, Wednesbury
SO 998956 ✻
Two tall brick engine houses, the earlier one with machicolated parapet, flank a boiler house on a railside site. The waterworks was established in 1871 by the South Staffordshire Waterworks Company which was formed in 1853 as one of the responses to the devastating cholera epidemic of 1848. The first beam engine was provided by James Watt & Co, and two more were added in 1876. It closed in 1976 and is now adapted for industrial units.

SA2 (Site of) **PATENT SHAFT COMPANY**
Leabrook Road, Wednesbury
SO 981947 **DEM** ✻
Iron gates with motifs are all that survives of the Patent Shaft & Axletree Company, founded in 1835 by the Rev James Hardy and a local grocer, Samuel Hodgetts. From small beginnings three huge works developed, extending to 13 acres and employing 4,000, world-famous for rolled sections, railway axles and wheels, and prefabricated bridges. Bessemer did some trials here, and in the C20th steelmaking dominated. Despite many attempts to stay competitive, the works closed in 1980.

SA3 (Site of) **BARROWS & HALL'S IRONWORKS**
Bloomfield, Tipton
SO 952933 ✻
At this works in 1825-32, John Hall developed the technique of 'pig-boiling' or 'wet puddling' which vastly improved on Cort's process. A Tipton Civic Society plaque on a modern office commemorates the invention. Boulton & Watt's first steam pumping engine was set to work here in 1776.

SA4 HARPER BEAN CAR FACTORY
Hurst Lane, Tipton Green
SO 949925 ✻
The site was developed by A Harper Sons and Bean Ltd as a fuse factory during the First War, and a modern car plant with assembly lines was planned on a massive scale in 1925. Completed chassis' were tested by driving them up to the Dudley factory (DU12) where the bodies were added.

SA5 FACTORY LOCKS
Factory Road, Tipton
SO 952926 **LSII** ✻
Three narrow locks built c.1829 by Telford where his New Line rises 20ft to join the Old Line of the Birmingham Canal. The bottom lock has an unusual cast iron footbridge cantilevered so as to leave a gap for towropes. Close to the top lock is a former boat gauging station, built 1873 in alternating courses of red and blue brick. Adjacent is a former boatmens' mission, and across the Old Line is a former stable block. The cast iron towpath bridge was provided by the Horseley Iron Co in 1848.

SA6 (Site of) **DUDLEY CASTLE ENGINE**
off Park Lane West, Tipton
SO 957916 **DEM** ■
From the minimal evidence available, Thomas Newcomen's first successful atmospheric or 'fire' engine (the 'Dudley Castle engine' of 1712)

SA4 Assembly line at the Bean car factory

was at the Coneygre Mine, close to the later crossing of the Birmingham Canal (Old Line) and the South Staffs Railway. The engine was moved to The Level near Brierley Hill c.1740, again to Broadwaters near Wednesbury by 1752, and subsequently scrapped.

SA7 CANAL EMBANKMENT AND AQUEDUCTS

Tipton and Dudley Port

SO 955926 to 984910 ❑

Telford's New Line was carried across upper Tame valley in Tipton by an arrow-straight embankment more than 2 miles long, pierced by aqueducts at Dudley Port. The Rylands Aqueduct (SO 968918) over Dudley Port Road (A461) has been replaced by a long concrete span, but Telford's structure survives as a very low bridge over East Park lane (SO 955919).

SA8 HORSELEY BRIDGE WORKS

Horseley Road, Tipton

SO 971924 ✻

The Horseley Coal & Iron Company was established here c.1780 and quickly became famous for many products including engines and bridges (eg., those cast for local canals). Some late-C19th erecting shops survive but re-roofed, next to the filled-in bed of the Toll End canal link.

SA9 'THE GREET BRIDGE'

Great Bridge

SO 978925 LSII ❑

Two stone arches built 1780 and later widened on the south side across the Greet Brook, a tributary of the River Tame. Only the north parapet can be seen from the road, built of stone with the marks of Tipton Parish and West Bromwich Parish.

SA10 RYDERS GREEN LOCKS

off Great Bridge Street

SO 980927 to 985917 **LSII** ✻

From Ryders Green Junction on the original Wednesbury Canal of 1769, eight narrow locks engineered by Smeaton and completed in 1786 take the Walsall Canal down to the Walsall Level at 408ft.

SA11 CANAL BRIDGES

Eagle Lane, Great Bridge

SO 977929 ❑

Eagle Lane crosses the Walsall Canal on a brick arch dated 1825 in cast Roman numerals. The north side of the South Staffordshire Railway (opened 1850) bridge has a cast beam and parapet formed of decorative cast panels.

SA12 SIDDONS NEW FOUNDRY

Howard Street, Golds Green

SO 987935 ✻

Joseph and Jesse Siddons, makers of cast enamelled hollowware, built this extensive new works in 1870-80. A series of parallel buildings with offices and a Works Engineer's house at the entrance, it is the most complete survival of a Black Country works of the period, though now used as industrial units.

SA13 W H KEYS OIL & TAR WORKS

Church Lane, West Bromwich

SP 002928 ■

The firm supplies oils and tar derivatives which are stored in a variety of old tanks, many of them formerly boilers including several of the egg-ended type.

SA14 GRAND JUNCTION AQUEDUCT

off Walsall Road, Hall Green

SP 017948 **LSII** ✻

A fine three-arch aqueduct of brick with iron railings carries the heavily engineered Tame Valley Canal of 1844 over the Grand Junction Railway of 1837. The canal embankment crossing the Tame valley was impressive until overshadowed by the M6, but there are still very impressive cuttings as the canal traverses Hall Green.

SA15 SANDWELL PARK FARM

off Salter's Lane, West Bromwich

SP 020914 **LSII** ❑

Early C19th planned farmstead on the Earl of Dartmouth's Sandwell Hall estate. A brick barn and arcaded cartsheds form three sides of a yard, with three-storey corner pavilions. Now a visitor centre.

SA16 IZONS FOUNDRY

Oldbury Road, Albion

SO 985910 ✻

This canalside zone was once the site of several ironworks, and some buildings including the offices of Izons & Co, established 1760 to manufacture cast and enamelled hollowware, survive as small factory units.

SA17 WEST BROMWICH INSTITUTE

Lodge Road, West Bromwich

SO 02915 ❑

Designed by Wood & Kenrick in brick and terracotta, opened 1886, providing facilities for arts, sciences, and technical instruction. Adjacent is the Ryland Memorial School of Art by the same architects, opened 1902, with a sculptured panel depicting various crafts.

SA18 COMMEMORATIVE STREET FURNITURE

High Street, West Bromwich

LSII ❑

The town has been generous with its memorials. Reuben Farley JP, a local coal and iron master, commemorated his mother Elizabeth by a highly decorative cast iron drinking fountain made by the Saracen Foundry of Glasgow, recently re-sited in the shopping

SA18 Reuben Farley's fountain at West Bromwich

centre (SP 007910) from Dartmouth Park. Close by is a cast iron clock of 1912 commemorat ng J Archibald Kenrick, and Farley himself is remembered in the Clock Tower at Carters Green (SO 997918), erected 1897 in red brick and terracotta, with a clock by Smiths of Derby.

SA19 DART SPRING COMPANY

Overend Street, West Bromwich

SP 009910 ✻

The company began on this site in 1895 as safe makers, became the Dart Spring and Safe Company by 1904, and separated the two sides of the business a few years later. Beh nd the prominently-named frontage the company specialises in automotive, railway and machinery springs.

SA20 WEST BROMWICH SPRING Co.

George Street, West Bromwich

SP 007907 ✻

Founded 1896 to produce a large variety of spring types from up to 3 inch diameter bar. The office frontage bears the name 'Helical Works' and stylised coil springs.

SA21 BROADWELL WORKS

Broadwell Road, Oldbury

SO 995897 ✻

The Oldbury Carriage & Wagon Company Ltd was formed in 1857 from Johnson & Kinder's railway rolling stock business which moved from Bromsgrove in 1854. In 1901 they became part of the Metropolitan Carriage, Wagon and Finance Co Ltd. The large workshops with prominent roof vents, now storage warehouses, are best seen from the railway; part of the office range in Broadwell Road has been demolished.

SA22 SPON LANE LOCKS

off Spon Lane, Smethwick

SO 999899 **LSII** ❑

A flight of three locks once on the Wednesbury line opened 1769, and now connecting the Old and New Lines at 473 and 453ft. They probably date from 1790 when Brindley's Smethwick summit level was lowered by Smeaton.

SA23 STEWARD AQUEDUCT

Spon Lane, Smethwick

SP 002898 **LSII** ❑

A two skew-arched brick aqueduct carrying Brindley's 1769/72 Old Line at 473ft over Telford's BCN New Line of 1826/28 at the 453ft level. The Old Line is crossed in turn by the LNWR Stour Valley line of 1854 and the whole is under the elevated M5 motorway built in the late 1960s on concrete stilts in and over the canal.

SA24 CHANCE'S GLASSWORKS

Spon Lane, West Bromwich

SP 005897 **LSII** ✻

The British Crown Glass Company established here c.1812 was bought by Henry Chance in 1824, and the sheet glass business introduced from France in 1832 attained fame in the contract for glazing the Crystal Palace in 1851. Equally famous was the 'Lighthouse Works' established to manufacture complex Fresnel-lensed lanterns which were exported all over the world. A seven-storey office block of 1847 and several warehouse ranges survive close to the canal (new line) together with two private bridges over it. The rest of the site is now a modern trading estate, its sign supported on two cast iron columns from the polishing shops

SA25 ARCHIBALD KENRICK & SONS

off Kenrick Way, West Bromwich

SP 007899 **LSII** ✻

A major foundry for domestic ironmongery, established c.1792 on the Birmingham Canal. The 3-storey gothic style brick office building, whose clock tower now rises above the elevated M5, has some terracotta details and dates from c.1890. The Shepherd castor was developed here in the 1950s.

SA26 GALTON BRIDGE

Roebuck Lane, Smethwick

SP 015893 **LSI** ❑

An outstanding cast iron bridge of 150ft span by Telford, 1829, over the New Line of the Birmingham Canal. Named after a BCN committee member, brick abutments with stone dressings support a lattice arch cast by the Horseley Iron Co. Now a footbridge. On the north side a massive single brick arch built 1789 by Smeaton (**SC**) crosses the improved Old line.

SA27 SMETHWICK PUMPHOUSE

Brasshouse Lane, Smethwick

SP 019890 **LSII** ❑ (occasionally)

Built 1892 between the Smeaton and Telford lines of the BCN, replacing two earlier pumping stations in the vicinity which raised water from the 453ft to the 473ft level. The two vertical compound engines with centrifugal pumps have long been removed, but the Galton Valley restoration programme has replaced one similar engine and built a new chimney.

SA28 TOLL HOUSE

High Street, Smethwick

SP 019888 **LSII** ✻

Known as 'The Blue Gates', from which a nearby inn and its successor took its name. Built c.1818 on the Birmingham-Oldbury-Dudley turnpike road of 1760/61. It was threatened with demolition for the Smethwick by-pass, but instead has been restored as an art centre.

SA29 ENGINE ARM AQUEDUCT

off Bridge Street, Smethwick

SP 023889 **SC** ❑

A fine cast iron aqueduct built c.1827 by Telford to carry the navigable Engine Arm feeder over the New Line. A cast trough on open ribs is flanked by twin towpaths carried on ribs with gothic-style lancets. Repaired and painted 1985. Accessible along towpath.

SA30 SMETHWICK LOCKS

Bridge Street, Smethwick

SP 026891 **LSII** ❑

The 473ft Wolverhampton level falls here to the 453ft Birmingham level. Brindley's original canal rose to 491ft here through six locks to cross the Smethwick summit, and Smeaton duplicated the bottom three locks when he dispensed with the high level and top three locks. Brindley's original locks were filled in 1960. At the junction of the Old and New Lines is a fine cast roving bridge by the Horseley Iron Works, 1828.

SA31 (Site of) SMETHWICK ENGINE

Bridge Street, Smethwick

SP 026888 ❑ (occasionally)

The site of Boulton & Watt's second pumping engine, supplied to the BCN in 1778. The engine was removed to Ocker Hill, Tipton in 1928 and subsequently to Birmingham's Museum of Science & Industry where it is occasionally steamed (BM14). The site was excavated in 1983-85 and special visits can be arranged.

SA32 TANGYE'S CORNWALL WORKS

Cornwall Road, Soho

SP 032891 ✻

Richard Tangye established himself in Birmingham in the 1850s and his business grew so fast that he moved in 1859 and again to the Cornwall Works in 1862. Tangye's famous hydraulic jack launched the Great Eastern and the company became famous for pumps, steam and gas engines, presses and machine tools. The company closed in the 1950s, but several large ranges of erecting sheds with cast round-head windows survive in mixed use on both sides of the road.

SA33 AVERY'S SOHO FOUNDRY

Foundry Lane, Soho

SP 036888 **LSII** ✻

On this site Boulton, Watt & Sons established their Soho Foundry in 1796 to provide and control the quality of steam engine parts. A row

SA29 Engine Arm aqueduct, Smethwick

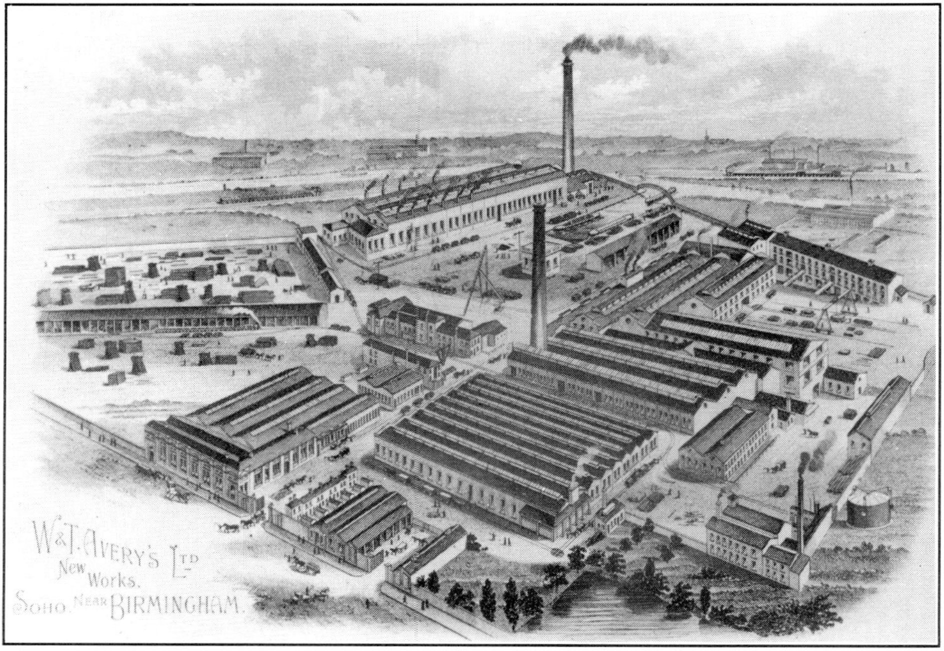

SA33 Avery's New Works at Soho

of early C19th cottages stood outside the foundry gates, and seven of these can still be seen through Avery's imposing C20th neo-classical style entrance arch. Inside the works the gates from James Watt's home at Heathfield Hall, and from the Liverpool Sailors' Home, have been re-erected.

SA33 Avery's Soho Foundry entrance

SA34 GKN WORKS
Heath Street, Smethwick
SP 036883 ✻
When Nettlefold & Chamberlain bought Sloane's patent for automatically cutting pointed woodscrews in 1854 they established a new factory here. The works expanded rapidly, especially in the late C19th, becoming part of the vast Guest, Keen & Nettlefold combine. The site is now in multiple occupation, but many buildings remain, with the characteristic alternating courses of red stretcher and blue header bricks; one such gable is dated 1897.

SA35 BANDSTAND
Lightwoods Park, Hagley Road West
LSII ❑
A late C19th bandstand, octagonal plan, cast columns and railings, an ogee dome of sheet iron; made by the Lion Foundry, Kirkintillock.

SA36 CHANCE MEMORIAL
West Smethwick Park, Victoria Rd, Smethwick
SP 007887 **LSII** ❑
Red brick and terracotta memorial on a granite base, unveiled 1897 in memory of James T Chance of Chance Bros, glass manufacturers.

SA37 LANGLEY MALTINGS
Western Road, Langley
SP 001891 **LSII** ✻
Two ranges of 3-storey maltings with six kilns, built 1870. Formerly Walter Showell & Sons,

they are still malting for Wolverhampton & Dudley Brewers (Banks and Hansons).

SA38 CANAL BRIDGE

Station Road, Langley

SO 996888 **LSII** ❑

The arch is carried on six cast iron segmental ribs bolted at the apex. It probably dates from 1837, later widened to accommodate footpaths.

SA39 OLDBURY LOCKS

off Tat Bank Road, Oldbury

SO 994888 **LSII** ❑

Six locks nicknamed 'The Crow' and still with single top and bottom gates raise the canal 38ft to the Titford Branch, the highest navigable level in England at 511ft OD. At the top is a junction with the Spon Lane branch (a feeder from Rotton Park Reservoir) and an engine house which once housed two beam engines recirculating 5 million gallons of water per day. All date from 1837/38.

SA40 ALBRIGHT & WILSON

Tat Bank, Oldbury

SO 992887 ✻

A large chemical works founded by Arthur Albright in 1851 to manufacture amorphous phosphorus, which was supplied in 1855 for the making of the first safety matches (in Sweden). Best seen from the elevated M5 which is the only view of the older buildings next to the nearly-filled Houghton's (Chemical) canal branch. Discarded retort pots have been used to build a wall at Shidas Lane (SO 984893).

SA41 JUNCTION INN

Birmingham Street, Oldbury

SO 991895 **LSII** ❑

The decorative lintels, brackets and string course are made of cast basalt from the Rowley quarries (SA46), melted under Henry Adcock's patent of c.1851 in the glass furnaces at Chance's Works nearby (SA24).

SA42 TITFORD POOLS

off Birchfield Lane, Whiteheath

SO 984881 ❑

Built c.1770 as a feeder reservoir for the Birmingham Canal, it became part of the canal system with the opening of Oldbury Locks (SA40) in 1837. Several branch canals serving colliery and brickworks wharves but now filled and built over, met here.

SA43 TIVIDALE AQUEDUCT

off East Tipton Road, Tividale

SO 968909 **LSII** ✻

Brindley's Old Line (1772) is carried over the Netherton Tunnel Branch by a two-arch aqueduct of blue brick, rebuilt in the 1890s. Adjacent are two canal company houses (BCN 174, 175) and the north portal of the Netherton Tunnel (**LSII**), 3027 yds long and the last canal tunnel of the canal age, built 1855-58 with 17ft waterway, two towpaths and gas lighting (DU22).

SA44 BRADES LOCKS

off Tividale Road, Tividale

SO 979904 **LSII** ❑

The half-mile Gower Branch (1836) connects the BCN New and Old Lines through three locks, the top two chambers forming the BCN's only staircase pair.

SA45 BIRMINGHAM NEW ROAD

(A4123)

SO 947918 to SP 012854 ❑

First proposed in 1908, and constructed as a four-lane road in 1924-27 with government aid for unemployment relief (DU7). One contemporary artist's impression shows it as a dual carriageway. A footbridge at SP 971903 once carried a tramway incline from Darby's Hill Quarry to canal wharves.

SA46 QUARRIES AT TURNER'S HILL

Rowley Regis

SO 966884 and 974890 areas ✻

The Rough Hills reflect an inlier of basalt which has been quarried since the mid-nineteenth century first for kerbs and setts, and later for crushed roadstone. Under a patent obtained by Henry Adcock c.1851, fused decorative building blocks were produced at Chance's Glass Works, and examples remain in the Birmingham area and at Oldbury (SA41). Quarry products were transported on inclined tramways to canal wharves on the Old Line and Dudley No 2 canals. The Turner's Hill Quarries are still active, but others have been filled and landscaped.

SA47 COBBS ENGINE HOUSE

Warrens Hall Park, Rowley Regis

SO 955883 **SC LSII** ❑

The surviving engine house contained a Watt type single-acting engine which worked from 1831; in 1873 it was taken over by the South

SA47 Cobb's Engine house, c.1929

Staffordshire Mines Drainage Commission and modified to the Cornish cycle with a 63" cylinder to drain 495,000 gallons per day from the surrounding coal mines. An adjacent engine house, now demolished, contained an atmospheric whim engine installed in 1832 but thought to date from c.1800. It was rejected by English museums, and acquired in 1930 by Henry Ford for his Dearborn museum, Chicago.

SA48 HINGLEYS SLAG HEAPS
Garratt's Lane, Old Hill
SO 959868 *
High banks of furnace slag on the north side of Garratt's Lane extend to Powke Lane where Noah Hingley's Netherton Ironworks were sited from 1838 to 1960. Hingley's installed the Black Country's first steam hammer in 1850, and was the last Black Country firm to make wrought iron in 1960. The concrete foundations of a slag crushing plant survive next to the dismantled Blowers Green—Old Hill railway branch.

SA49 FIRE STATION
Halesowen Road, Old Hill
SO 955864 *
A fine example of a small local authority fire station, inscribed *Rowley Regis U.D.C. 1903* above the former double doors. Behind is a tall hose drying and look-out tower. Now a shop.

SA50 DAVID WILLETTS CHAIN WORKS
Upper High Street, Cradley Heath
SO 948864 *
A two-storey building and open yard with the remains of lean-to open fronted chainshops surrounding it. The company closed in 1970, and the site is now used as small industrial units.

SA51 CHAINSHOP
Bannister Street, Cradley Heath
SO 947865 *
A rare surviving example of a typical outworker chainshop, with four hearths. A few years ago one hearth was still complete with its treadle 'tommy hammer'. Used as a store.

SA52 JOSEPH WOODHOUSE CHAINWORKS
80 Foxoak Street, Cradley Heath
SO 944862 *
Single-storey workshops surrounding a yard behind a large house. Founded in the late C19th to make small chain, later electrically welded chain. Name and order book acquired 1991 by Griff Chains Ltd of Mushroom Green (DU28) who transferred their electrically welded chain manufacture here.

SA53 CHAINSHOP
Bank Street, Cradley Heath
SO 944862 *
A rare two-storey womens' chainshop, with forge chimneys front and rear, can be seen behind No 15, a small subsided cottage 'pulled by the pits'. Across the street is another two-storey workshop, probably a former chain-shop but now a steel fabricator.

SA54 THEATRE ROYAL
Bank Street, Cradley Heath
SO 945861 *
Opened 1912 as a theatre, later converted to a cinema but retaining a prominent fly tower. Closed 1988, the fine interior still intact.

SA55 ROWLAND PRIEST WORKS
Lower High St, Cradley Heath
SO 940858 *
Two-storey brick workshops surrounding a yard, established 1877 for the manufacture of pulley blocks and extended c.1891. The south gable and painted wall panels still catalogues many of the products.

SA56 STOUR VALE WORKS
Woods Lane, Cradley Heath
SO 941856 *
Henry Wood & Co, chainmakers, were established at Lye in 1780 and in 1847 his sons built this very large works. In 1871 J Wood, Aston & Co began making anchors, but this lasted only a few years. The western section became part of Griffin-Woodhouse chainmakers (established c.1880) who still have a small works in Woods Lane, and the eastern part became a galvanising works. Ernest Stevens, makers of 'Judge Ware' enamelled utensils, occupied buildings on both sides of Woods Lane and is still active on the north side. The whole site is now an industrial estate, but the long ranges of brick buildings with prominent louvred roof vents are still impressive.

SA57 CRADLEY BOILER WORKS
Woods Lane, Cradley Heath
SO 941857 *
The company moved from Cookley (Kidderminster) to this site in 1875. A brick boiler erecting tower survives in a range of large buildings, but a second, wooden one has been demolished.

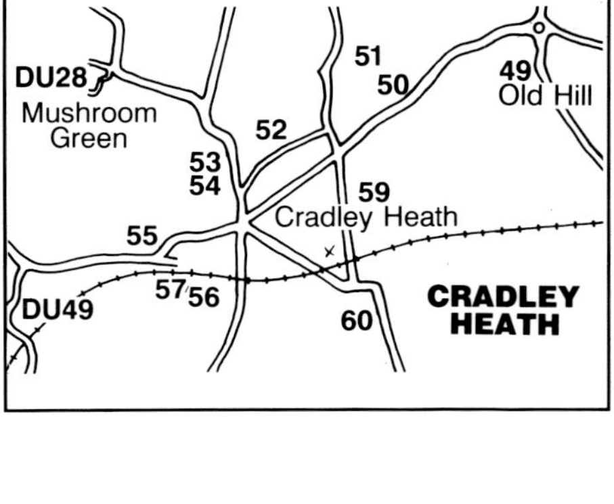

SA57 Boiler erecting tower, Cradley Boiler Works

SA58 EAGLE CHAINWORKS
Corngreaves Road, Cradley Heath
SO 947858 ✻
Developed from a six-hearth chainshop founded by Samuel Woodhouse in 1870. Probably the first in Britain to introduce electrically welded steel chain in 1903. Employed the last woman chainmaker, Lucy Woodhall, who retired in 1973. A family firm until 1983, went into voluntary liquidation in 1988, but the site remains unaltered.

SA59 LLOYDS CHAIN TEST HOUSE
Corngreaves Road, Cradley Heath
SO 947858 ✻
Established c.1860, one of many testing centres to cope with load testing of locally made chain. Later used by Premier Tubes Ltd. The very large brick building with paired elliptical-headed windows is surrounded by modern sheds, but is still impressive.

SA60 CORNGREAVES IRONWORKS
Corngreaves Road, Cradley Heath
SO 947855 ✻
An ironworks founded by James Attwood c.1780, and sold to the British Iron Co in 1826. It became the centre of a vast complex of mines and connecting tramways working a 560 acre mineral estate. Sold July 1893, the two furnaces have long since gone but some nondescript buildings survive. The company school built 1848/9 for the children of its workforce at Plant Street (SO 948864) survives.

SA61 BIRMINGHAM GUN BARREL WKS
Hayseech, Old Hill
SO 959850 **LSII** ✻
A rare survivor of the once common water powered sites along the Stour, now tastefully converted to small industrial units. The former pool, water from which turned 6ft (1•9m) diameter grindstones, is now a car park, but part of the dam is visible.

SA62 METHODIST CHAPEL
Hayseech, Old Hill
SO 959851 ✻
Built 1870 on land 'begged from Mr Burr of the Gunbarrel Works', supposedly on the site where John Wesley preached in March 1770:
John Wesley rode a boony 'oss with eyes as black as sin—we took 'im up tew Hayseech Brook an throwed 'im yed fust in!

SA52 Joseph Woodhouse chainworks

SA60 Corngreaves furnaces, *see previous page*

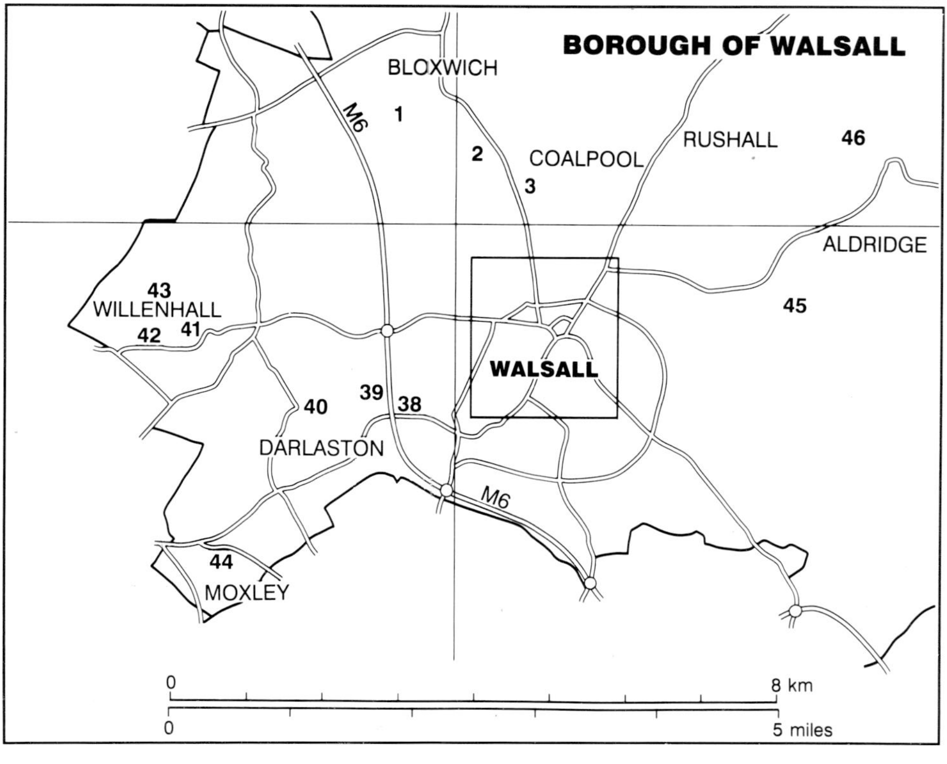

BOROUGH OF WALSALL

Walsall is the capital of the English leather goods industry, a trade which grew up over centuries to cater for every conceivable item relating to horses. The metal workers were first, for c.1540 Leland remarked on the number of smiths and bit-makers at work. Like other places, this may have been part-time work, but lorinery—saddlers ironmongery and the metal parts of harness—became the town's speciality. The leather side of horse harness began to appear in the mid-C18th, and by 1800 saddle making was taking root. The war in Europe and the growth of wheeled carriages brought an enormous development in horse furniture, and by the mid-C19th Walsall was supplying the world. The peak years were 1850 to 1880, with Australia and South America being the best markets. In this period too the cart gear trade developed. But after 1918 as the horse was overtaken by the motor car Walsall switched to the fancy leather goods trade.

Walsall was characterised by small specialist leather and harness makers, and the central area of the town was once packed with workshops in houses and built behind houses. In the second half of the C19th many factories were purpose-built, but most of these were still on a scale which fits the intimate tightly packed streets of the town. The edge of the coalfield passed west of the town centre, and Walsall's coal mines and ironworks lay to the west and north-east, linked by the amazing meanders of the Wyrley & Essington Canal. The town was also famous for lime, mined at depth to the east and under the town itself, to the great anxiety of some present householders; the lake in the Arboretum is a drowned former mine entrance. To the north-east, between Aldridge and Walsall Wood, the land is ravaged by brick clay digging. Beyond this lie Brownhills and the fringes of the Cannock Coalfield, which have been excluded from this guide.

Boundary changes brought Darlaston and Willenhall into Walsall. The former's heavy engineering works and fastenings trade have almost disappeared, but Willenhall's lock trade, allied with Wolverhampton rather than Walsall, involves large and small firms including Squire, Union and Yale.

WA1 DELAVILLE SPELTER WORKS

Leamore Lane, Bloxwich

SJ 993016 ✻

One furnace chimney amongst modern buildings marks this canal-side zinc smelting works established in 1901. A building which still contained two coal-fired reverberatory furnaces was demolished in 1991.

WA2 HATHERTON WORKS

Leamore Lane, Leamore

SK 010003 ✻

A 3-storey works, 'L'-shaped plan dating from c.1910, brick with steeply pitched tiled roof. A rare example outside the town centre, still producing leather goods.

WA3 AQUEDUCT

off Forest lane, Leamore

SK 005009 ✻

The Wyrley & Essington Canal is carried at full width in a cast iron trough, of six sections bolted together with a narrow brick pier between the tracks, over the LNWR Cannock branch. The towpath is carried on a cast segmental beam, with the inscription *Lloyds Foster & Co, Engineers, Wednesbury, 1856*.

WA4 BOATMENS' REST

Birchills

SP 005995 **CA** ❑

Built 1900 of brick with paired lancet windows of cast iron and an ornate roof vent, one of three provided by the Midland District of the Seamen and Boatmen's Friend Society, with kitchen and coffee room on the ground floor and a large meeting room above for concerts, services and a Sunday School.

WA5 WALSALL CANAL LOCKS

off Wolverhampton Road, Walsall

SP 005986 to 005995 **LSII CA** ❑

A flight of eight locks completed 1841, connecting the Walsall Canal with the Wyrley & Essington Canal. A keeper's cottage, (BCN 206, **LSII**) by the top lock has an octagonal-fronted toll office attached.

WA6 CO-OPERATIVE BOOT REPAIRING FACTORY

64 Hollyhedge Lane, Walsall

SP 004989 ✻

A compact two-storey works with prominent loading bay, built for the local Co-op society; now a cash and carry, formerly leather dealers.

WA4 and WA5 Walsall top lock and Boatmen's Rest

WA7 WALSALL MALLEABLE IRON CO.
Wolverhampton Road, Walsall
SP 003988 *
The foundry developed in the mid-C19th, making a range of small lorinery, lock and builders ironmongery. It continued to work in amazingly derelict buildings until recently. The 2-storey corner building was an office and fettling workshop, and the tall chimney served the annealing oven. There is still a traditional two-man tub casting shop at the back of the works.

WA8 ALBION CORN MILL
Wolverhampton Street, Walsall
SP 005988 **CA** *
A fine four-storey brick steam mill built 1848. The central archway once extended over a public road, and there was a covered canal dock as well as a private coal wharf.

WA9 RELIANCE WORKS
72 Farringdon Street, Walsall
SO 006992 *
A 2-storey 'L'-shaped workshop range, purpose-built as a whip manufactory for Edward Goddard Ltd, the Eegee Whip Company. The frontage blends with the adjacent domestic property.

WA10 CROWN WORKS
Algernon Street, Walsall
SP 009988 *
A long two-storey multi-windowed works in plain brick, built 1887, with a cart arch and two cottages. Formerly a leather goods manufacturers, later making leather gloves, and now the Ideal Saddle Company.

WA11 CENTAUR WORKS
5-8 Green Lane, Walsall
SP 011987 *
Purpose-built c.1910 for Albert Jagger Ltd, coach and saddlers' ironmongers. with a ground-floor elevation of futuristic terracotta. The firm survived by diversifying into fittings for the motor trade. Next door the Salvation Army Citadel, built 1902, boldly proclaims repentance.

WA12 WHEWAY BECKER LTD
72 Long Acre Street, Walsall
SP 008992 *
An extensive works with office on Green Lane and C20th workshops, the company still manufactures hames, a purpose for which it was originally established.

WA13 HOOPER, HUCKER & CO
52 Short Acre Street, Walsall
SO 010991 *
Some buildings have been demolished at this once cluttered site, but there are still several single and 3-storey buildings, and a black chimney emblazoned with 'Hucker'. Still in use as a currier's.

WA14 VICTORIA CORN MILLS
Long Acre Street / Stafford Road, Walsall
SP 010993 *
A small three-storey steam corn mill, brick with cast iron windows, built 1845 by J E Dolman. Now converted to workshops.

WA15 Leather workshops, Walsall Leather Centre

WA15 LEATHER CENTRE
56-57 Wisemore, Walsall
SP 012989 ❑
A fine range of 3-storey workshops with ranges extending behind to enclose two courtyards. Formerly a leatherworks, and now the Walsall Leather Centre which incorporates a trade and educational element, and a museum of the local industry.

WA16 ALBION TANNERY
7 Hatherton Street, Walsall
SP 015988 to 015992 *
A much altered but now rare example of a tannery built c.1900, formerly Stokes & Co, tanners, curriers and japanners. Close by, 21-23, a small works developed by amalgamating adjacent properties, still makes bridles.

WA17 BROOKS & ORTON LTD
Littleton Street West, Walsall
SP 015990 *
Disappointingly, this is not a tannery. The long building with wooden louvres is a timber store, and other buildings house a sawmill and offices.

WA18 GLOBE WORKS
Lower Forster Street, Walsall
SP 017989 *
The imposing works of Jabez Cliff & Co Ltd, once saddlers and now producing fancy leather goods. Nearby is a small domestic works formerly a curriers and dressers, now the office of Beebee & Beebee Ltd, saddletree makers.

WA19 HULME & SONS
13 Cecil Street, Walsall
SP 016994 *
A double-fronted house with workshops behind, end-on to terraced houses, formerly a covered buckle works and now manufacturing fancy leather goods. Next door was another leather works, part of which has been demolished and the remainder neatly converted into flats.

WA20 IMPERIAL LEATHER WORKS
Butts Lane, Walsall
SP 017994 *
An ornate works built in two phases, once making saddlery, harness and fancy goods and until recently used by John Hatherill Stephenson Ltd, leather goods makers; currently for sale as offices/manufacturing space.

WA21 THE ARBORETUM
Lichfield Street, Walsall
SP 019991 **CA** ❑
The lake is a former limestone quarry and limestone mine which was flooded by 1845. In 1874 the Walsall Arboretum and Lake Company opened the present park, now famous for its mature broad-leaf woods and its Autumn illuminations.

WA22 Various works
Marsh Street, Walsall
SP 010985 *
Close to the canal basin and railway station in the town centre, Marsh Street was once lined on both sides by leather trade buildings, and those which survive show evidence of many changing uses. Still in good condition are: **Crown Works**, an impressive frontage with brick pilasters and a variety of window styles. Built as a bridle cutter's, but now occupied by Whitehouse, Cox & Co, makers of fancy leather goods.

24, Greatrex House, workshop ranges behind a rather plain 3-storey brick frontage with loading bays, now making luxury leather goods.

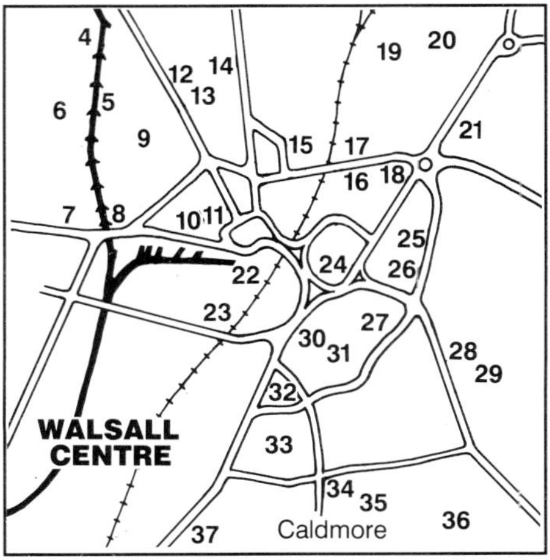

WA23 Various works
Station Street, Walsall
SP 009983 to 101985 *

Virtually all the buildings were used by the leather trade at one time, but now there is more variety. Gulleys (entrances) from the street frontage lead to a common access back street with workshops, some of which are now in separate use; one houses a bridle maker. At the south end is the massive five-storey block of the **Ravenscraig Works** of Boak (Walsall) Ltd, the town's largest curriers. Next door the premises of **L B Parkes Anodising** use former domestic premises as offices, with extensive workshop ranges behind which can best be seen from Marsh Street.

WA24 TOWN HALL CHAMBERS
21 Leicester Street, Walsall
SP 013986 **CA** *

Part of a commercial development close to the new Town Hall, with shops, offices and a massive five-storey harness and saddlery works (W Brookes & Sons). No 9 which has housed saddlers' ironmongers and leather goods makers, is still a saddlery.

WA25 BREWERY TOWER
off Lower Rushall Street. Walsall
SP 017987 *

Behind a pub recently renamed 'Katz' is a small 3-storey plus basement brick tower brewery, very successfully converted to a dwelling.

WA26 PRICE EYLAND WORKS
Lower Rushall Street, Walsall
SP 016986 **LSII** *

Several domestic properties including two once fine mid-eighteenth century houses front extensive ranges of workshops, all derelict since 1985 when the business moved elsewhere. Established 1760 as buckle makers, the com-

WA23 Boak's Ravenscraig Works, Walsall

pany made millions of leather and webbing straps on army contracts.

WA27 36/37 GOODALL STREET
Walsall
SP 016983 **CA** *

Two shops flank a cart entrance leading to workshops facing each other across a narrow brick-paved yard, all nicely refurbished as speciality shop units. Across the road is the Art School, exemplifying the provision of decorative arts training in a manufacturing town.

WA28 WALSALL BOX COMPANY
Bank Street, Walsall
SP 019983 *

A complex of different ages and styles, from a 2-storey brick office through 3 and 4-storey workshops including a 1930s building with reinforced concrete panels. Makes a variety of cardboard boxes.

WA29 JOSEPH CARVER LTD
44 Eldon Street, Walsall
SP 019982 *

A three-storey brick building dated 1891 with extensive premises behind, the former 'Steam Whip Works' of Joseph Carver Ltd, the town's leading whip makers established 1776. Only half the planned frontage was built. David Carver built a car in 1902 and began the engineering side which continues elsewhere.

WA30 No 13A BRADFORD STREET
Walsall
SP 012983 **CA** *

The ultimate in hideaway sites, two narrow doorways between a shops and a pub give access to a small works which has made harness furniture, saddles, fancy leather goods and now baby reins (the Teach-to-Walk Manufacturing Co). The pub has a nice frontage in blue and brown tiles.

WA31 JOHN SHANNON & SONS LTD
George Street, Walsall
SP 014983 **CA** ✳
The most imposing industrial building in Walsall, the frontage built 1887 in three phases, four tall storeys in brick with large windows, and with extra storeys at the rear as the land slopes away. The whole is dominated by large roof vents and two towers with water tanks. John Shannon came from Scotland to start a drapery business in 1826.

WA32 Various works
Mountrath Street, Walsall
SP 012982 ✳
No 10 is a small former leather workshop on a triangular site, rather run-down. **No 12** is a range of smart 2-storey workshops now used as clothing manufacturers. Nearby streets have some very small 2-storey workshops, now in different uses.

WA33 Various works
Glebe Street, Walsall
SP 011979 to 013979 ✳
A number of leather trade works built integral with or as extensions to domestic properties; the best examples are:
No 6; a former bit, spur and stirrup works, now Goodall Leather Goods Ltd. **No 72**; a purpose-built works amongst domestic properties, until recently in use by Walsall Purse Co.
No 82; a terraced works with ornate stone entrance door and large extensions to the rear, It was used by Frederick Wich (Walsall) Ltd making leather goods until recently.

WA34 COTTAGES
1-5 Little Caldmore, Walsall
SP 013988 ✳
A row of leather workers' cottages built c.1800, recently restored.

WA35 Various works
Bath Road/Bath Street, Walsall
SP 014975 to 014979 ✳
A fine concentration of leather-related sites, including: **Holland House** (51-57); a fine two-storey brick frontage with a stone plaque, 'Bath Street Works, 1800', clearly showing expansion over adjacent sites; formerly a buckle and harness works.
Glebeland Works (59); an imposing two and three-storey works frontage showing three clear phases of development, and with extensive workshops behind. Formerly a bridle cutter's.
No 27a; a good example of a detached workshop behind domestic property. **Excelsior Works**; a two-storey brick building on a corner site with corner entrance, formerly a saddlers' ironmongers.

WA31 John Shannon's clothing factory, Walsall

WA36 HIGHGATE BREWERY
Sandymount Road, Walsall
SP 017986 **LSII** ✳
Established by the Fletcher family in 1898, and sold to Mitchells and Butlers in 1939. A good example of a Victorian brewery, still producing the fine dark Highgate mild.

WA37 PARAGON WORKS
Wednesbury Road, Walsall
SP 010978 to 009977 ✳
No 47-49, a fine three-storey works with a terracotta panel proclaiming its date (1902) and purpose (saddles and harness). It has recently been converted to flats, with insensitive win-

WA35 Glebeland Works

dows. **No 17** is a low two-storey works on a corner site, used variously for the making of harness furniture and fancy goods.

WA38 TRAMWAY GENERATING STATION

Darlaston Road, Walsall

SO 993976 ✻

The South Staffordshire Tramways Co was one of the first to adopt electric traction from overhead, on January 1st 1893. This canal-side generating station had three compound steam engines driving an Elwell-Parker dynamo, the electrical equipment provided by the Electric Construction Co of Bushbury, Wolverhampton. Trams ceased in 1930 but the station has been restored and now houses a wine wholesaler.

WA39 JAMES BRIDGE AQUEDUCT

Bentley Mill Way, Darlaston

SO 989978 **LSII** ❑

The Walsall Canal, completed 1799, crosses the lane on two squat brick arches, one badly distorted. The nearby aqueduct over the River Tame has been replaced by concrete culverts.

WA40 IMPERIAL BOLT & NUT WORKS

Lower Green, Darlaston

SO 980976 ✻

A long, derelict frontage proclaims *Charles Richards & Son Ltd. Estd 1870. Imperial Bolt & Nut Works. Extn 1936* in glazed brick. There were several bolt and nut works in this district.

WA41 EXCELSIOR LOCK WORKS

68 Wood Street, Willenhall

SO 966987 ✻

A former house now serves as office and warehouse, with 2-storey workshop and very narrow single-storey lean-to sheds in the yard behind. Still working and well maintained. Close by, behind a derelict double-fronted house, is a tall 2-storey workshop with windows all round, now an engineering workshop. Not far away is the large Yale factory, and in Cemetery Road South it is difficult to distinguish domestic and industrial premises.

WA42 NATIONAL LOCK MUSEUM

New Road, Willenhall

SO 962984 **LSII** ❑

The museum was established in 1985 in a house with lockmaker's workshop across the yard, now restored for demonstrations. The house contained a draper's shop until c.1980, and is now furnished in period style with exhibitions on the local lock-making industry.

WA43 WORKSHOP

27 Temple Bar, Willenhall

SO 863991 ✻

There were formerly many small workshops in the town, all engaged in the lock trade. This yard has two 2-storey workshops, one with a pitched roof seemingly running the wrong way. Now a small engineering works.

WA44 CANAL BRIDGE

under Church Street, Moxley.

SO 968958 ✻

Telford's Holyhead Road (now A41) crosses the Walsall Canal (1799) on a high brick skew arch, which has been widened by the addition of girders and a parapet of rivetted plates to accommodate a footpath.

WA45 HAY HEAD LIME WORKS

off Longwood Lane, Aldridge

SP 044990 **CP** ❑

The Wenlock limestones were exploited here in underground mines, and John Wilkinson took an interest, as a source for his furnaces at Bradley. The Wyrley & Essington built its Daw End Branch to the mines in 1800. The canal's terminal basin, together with foundations of headstocks and a pumping engine, can be traced in woodland. Nearby (SP 039991) the Rushall Canal (completed in 1847) begins its fall through nine locks to join the Tame Valley Canal, close to the M6.

WA46 ALDRIDGE BRICKWORKS

Brickyard Road, Aldridge

SK 045023 ✻

The whole of this area was mined for coal in the late C19th, after which a line of brickworks extracted clay from huge surface pits. The pits now provide landfill sites and most of the works—Atlas, Springfield, Empire, Northywood, Victoria—have gone, but Ibstock still operate the modernised Aldridge Brickworks. The small canal basin once served this and Aldridge Colliery, (some buildings survive at SK 047024). At SK 049026 a huge pit cuts the line of the Midland Railway's Walsall Wood Branch, closed 1930, leaving overbridges stranded both sides.

WA44 Holyhead Road canal bridge, Moxley

Wolverhampton itself lies outside the tight definition of the Black Country, but from time to time it has been called the capital of the Black Country. The town centre ***by a fortunate geological accident*** lies north of faults limiting the coalfield, but extensions of the borough's administrative boundaries, particularly in 1966 when Bilston was annexed, have given it a large slice of land re-used after the devastation of mining and ironworking.

Wolverhampton's early importance was as a general market and wool market, but by the late eighteenth century freedom from guild restrictions had encouraged industry based on coal and iron. A specialist trade in lock and keys was developing by the mid C17th (in 1801 a directory lists 163 locksmiths), and steel buckles became important in the C18th. Tinplate and japanning were

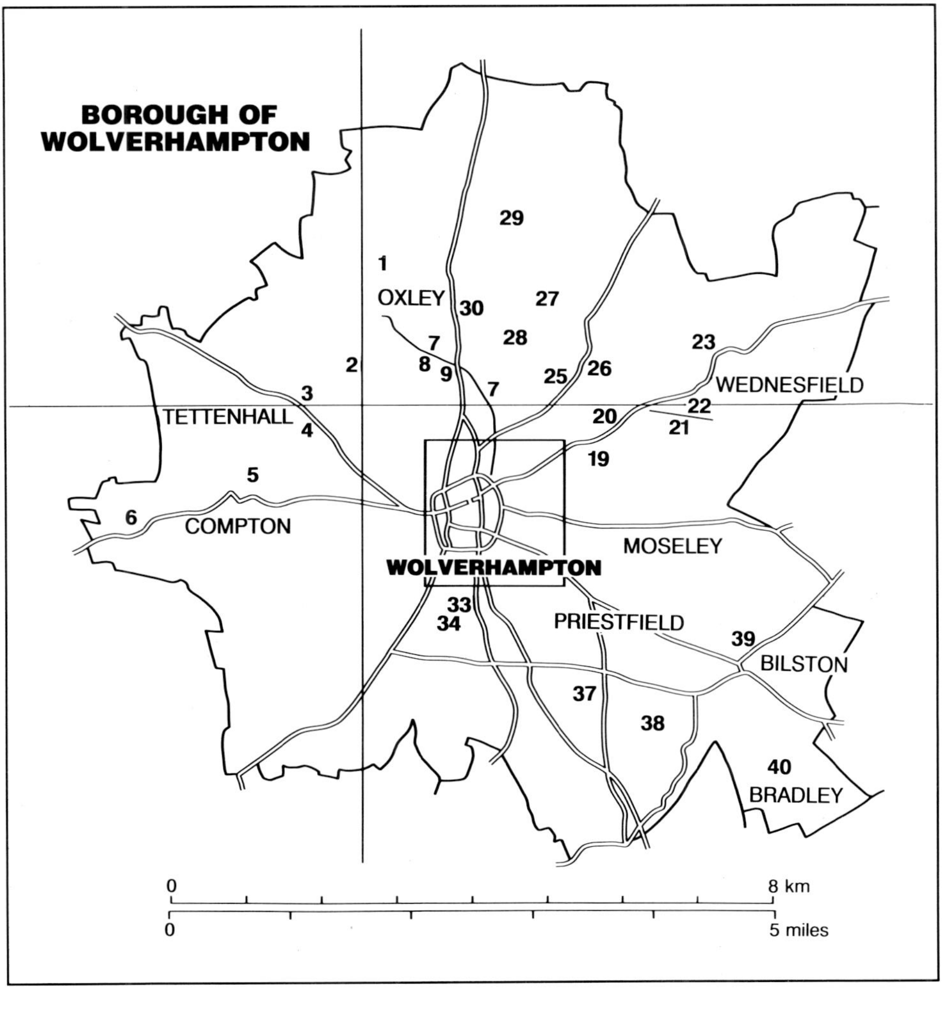

introduced from Pontypool (S Wales) c.1720, and in the nineteenth century there were many companies making the whole range of tinwares from trunks to tableware, tinned, galvanised and japanned. From the 1860s many companies began to make bicycles, stimulating the tube industry; Rudge began here and Sunbeam and Wearwell became famous for quality. Cycle making led to early experiments with cars, and several companies enjoyed some years' success, Sunbeam being the best known through its racing exploits. Motor cycle making—AJS and Villiers—was only slightly more successful, but motor component manufacture has remained important. Railway engineering came to the town in the 1850s and electrical engineering was important from the 1880s.

Wolverhampton shares with Willenhall (part of Walsall MBC) the near monopoly of the British lock trade, and in Wednesfield the making of keys was an important outwork industry. Wednesfield had its own exclusive industry, the making of animal traps which were exported world-wide. South and east of Wolverhampton lay the mining districts, their canals lined with ironworks and foundries; John Wilkinson built his first Black Country furnace at Bradley in 1757-58, and the last furnace, 'Elizabeth' at Bilston Steel Works, was demolished in 1980. In contrast, Bilston became and remains famous for the art of enamelling.

WN1 AUTHERLEY CANAL JUNCTION

off Aldersley Road, Oxley

SJ 902020 ❏

A stop lock with a fall of six inches (150mm) separates Telford's Birmingham & Liverpool Junction Canal (completed 1838) from Brindley's Staffordshire & Worcestershire Canal of 1772. There is a wide skew roving bridge (**LSII**) and an octagon fronted tollhouse.

WN2 WATER BRIDGE

off Aldersley Road, Dunstall

SJ 007898 **LSII** ❏

The summit level of the Staffs and Worcs. Canal passes through a shallow cutting, over which a wide brick arch carries a track and the Smestow Brook. The S&W cast number plate (No 63) names it as 'Tunstall' Bridge.

WN3 THE ROCK

Tettenhall Road, Newbridge

SJ 891001 ❏

An embankment and deep rock cutting through the steep western side of the Smestow valley originate in Telford's remodelling of the Holyhead road in the 1820s. Old Hill marks the former alignment.

WN4 RAILWAY STATION AND YARD

Henwood Road, Newbridge

SO 891998 ❏ ✱

A station on the Wombourn Branch which opened as late as 1925, closing to passengers in 1932 and to goods in 1965. Part of the station was restored in 1984 and the goods shed is used by a roofing contractor.

WN7 Bottom lock of the Wolverhampton flight

WN5 COMPTON LOCK
off Henwood Road, Compton
SO 884989 ❑
Here the Staffs and Worcs Canal begins its long descent down the Smestow valley to the Severn. Reputed to be Brindley's first lock.

WN6 WIGHTWICK MANOR
Wightwick Bank
SO 868985 **LSII★ NT**
A mock-Tudor mansion designed 1887 by Edward Ould for Theodore Mander, proprietor of the paint and varnish business which was established in 1775. An east wing, also by Ould, was added in 1895, and the house contains many original features by William Morris and the Pre-Raphaelites.

WN7 WOLVERHAMPTON CANAL LOCKS
SJ 903012 to SO 917991 ❑
Brindley's Birmingham Canal rose 133ft (40m) from sylvan surroundings at Aldersley Junction through 20 locks to the centre of Wolverhampton. The bottom lock was later replaced by two to make 21. There is a toll cottage by the top lock.

WN8 OXLEY VIADUCT
over Gorsebrook Road, Oxley
SJ 910006 ✻
Built by Robert Stephenson and William Baker for the Shrewsbury & Birmingham Railway, 1847-49, an early use of Staffordshire blue brick. Another viaduct carries the line, opened 1852, from High Level Station to the original Grand Junction line which bypassed Wolverhampton.

WN9 STAFFORD ROAD WORKS MEMORIAL
Gorsebrook Road, Oxley
SJ 912005 ❑
A plaque and set of wheels commemorates the Stafford Road Works of the Shrewsbury & Birmingham, later Great Western Railway. Standard gauge locomotives were built from 1859 to 1908; the Works closed in 1964 and has been totally demolished.

WN10 VICTORIA INTERCHANGE BASIN
off Lock Street, Wolverhampton
SO 917992 ❑
Formerly a rail-served canal basin, opened 1849 for the transfer of traffic between the Birmingham Canal and the Shrewsbury & Birmingham Railway. The GWR developed its Herbert Street goods station adjacent; the basin was filled in 1931, but the large goods sheds survived in railway use to 1967. Now a builders' merchants.

WN11 ART GALLERY AND MUSEUM
Lichfield Street
SO 914988 **LSII** ❑
Designed by J A Chatwin and opened 1884 in conjunction with the town's International Exhibition of Arts and Manufactures of that year. The Bath stone building has external Portland stone friezes by Boulton of Cheltenham, depicting arts, sciences, and strong references to the local industries of metal working and lock making. The statue of Prince Albert in Queens Square was unveiled by Queen Victoria in 1866, during her first public appearance after his death.

WN12 Chubb's Lock and Safe Works

WN12 CHUBBS LOCK & SAFE WORKS
Fryer Street
SO 917989 *

Charles and Jeremiah Chubb began making locks at Portsmouth, but moved to Horseley Fields in 1818 on patenting his 'detector' lock. The firm occupied various buildings there including the former workhouse from 1840, until moving to this purpose-built works in 1899. The imposing 6-storey brick building, its name proudly emblazoned in white glazed brick, is currently being refurbished and extended as a media centre, the company having occupied a new factory in Wednesfield Road since 1938.

WN13 THE QUEEN'S BUILDING
Victoria Square
SO 917988 **LSII** *

The offices and boardroom of the Shrewsbury & Birmingham Railway Co, by Edward Banks and opened October 1849. From 'The Railway Arches' a carriage driveway led to the first High Level station. Used as a District Goods Manager's Office from 1860 to 1960; now restored for a bus travel enquiry office.

WN14 OLD STEAM MILL
Cornhill
SO 920988 *

A steam mill established here c.1800 was rebuilt after a fire in 1851 by William Fairbairn, reputedly the first building to employ wrought iron beams in fireproof construction. Externally brick with sandstone gable pediments and gutter, its four storeys are much altered It occupies a cramped site between the canal and the high level (LNWR) railway, and has been worked by J N Miller for more than a century. Across the road is a stable block and the large LNWR goods shed, once straddling a canal arm.

WN15 LOW LEVEL RAILWAY STATION
Sun Street
SO 921988 **LSII** *

Built by three railway companies which became part of the GWR, it opened incomplete in 1854 with an overall roof and mixed gauge tracks. Broad gauge trains ceased in 1869 and the roof was removed in 1934. Intercity trains were diverted to High Level in 1967 and the station closed in 1972. Bought by the Council and partially restored by MSC labour in 1986-88, but now neglected.

WN16 TWIN BORE TUNNELS
Horseley Fields, Wolverhampton
SO 923987 *

To the south of Low Level station the Oxford, Worcester & Wolverhampton Railway passed under the Wyrley & Essington Canal and various works in parallel single-bore tunnels built 1852-54. Tracks lifted in 1973. Seen from Mill Street bridge.

WN17 ELECTRICITY GENERATING STATION
Commercial Road, Horseley Fields
SO 923982 ❑

An impressive brick building with one decorative gable of terracotta, it was opened in 1895 with equipment by Thomas Parker's Electric Construction Company whose works were in Stafford Road. Coal came to a canal basin at the rear. The station was extended in 1936, went out of use in the 1950s and the power hall now houses a timber merchant. The inscription *Wolverhampton Municipal Electric Light & Power Station* crosses two gables.

WN18 RAILWAY GOODS WAREHOUSE
Wednesfield Road
SO 922990 *

The site was intended to be the Midland Railway's passenger station after 1878, but running powers to High Level Station were retained and the large goods shed was completed in 1881. Disused since 1988.

WN19 RAILWAY TUNNEL
Two Bridges, off Wednesfield Road
SO 932995 *

The Grand Junction Railway, opened 1837, passes under the Wyrley & Essington Canal (1795) by a 180yd (160m) tunnel. The Midland Railway's line from Walsall crosses the canal directly above. Nothing remains of Wolverhampton's original Wednesfield Heath station (GJR), north-west of the tunnel.

WN20 STEEL-FRAMED HOUSES
Coronation Road, Heath Town
SO 934998 *

The houses at the south end, and the adjoining Lawrence Avenue, were built in the late 1920s on the 'Dennis-Wild' system, with a steel frame clad in brick or timber rendered over. Re-clad and refurbished in the late 1980s.

WN21 WEDNESFIELD LOCKS
off Wolverhampton Road, Wednesfield
SO 939999 to 948998 *

The Bentley Canal was opened in 1843 to provide a short link between Walsall and Wolverhampton. Abandoned in 1961, there is a fine cast roving bridge at the junction and two derelict locks can still be seen amidst desolation.

WN22 GRAISLEY WORKS
Rookery Street, Wednesfield
SJ 942001 *

The 2-storey building in dark brick was a manure works, grinding basic slag from local furnaces for its phosphate content. Later it became part of W G Sidebotham's animal trap

WN24 Mitchell and Butler's Springfield Brewery

works, established c.1913. This closed in 1981 and all but a small section has been rebuilt at the Black Country Museum (DU10).

WN23 KEY WORKSHOP
Amos lane, Wednesfield
SJ 946007 *
An ivy-covered 2-storey brick workshop, still in use by J Mattox & Co, a survivor of the once extensive local industry of key-making.

WN24 SPRINGFIELD BREWERY
Cambridge Street
SO 919993 *
William Butler established a brewery at this site in 1873 with a capacity of 350 barrels per week. It was enlarged in 1882/4 and again in 1895, when the cooperage was added at the west end of the site, and a stableyard was built across the road. The ornate canopied entrance (**LSII**) dates from this rebuilding and the brewing tower retains its copper mash tuns.

WN25 HENRY MEADOWS LTD
Cannock Road, Park Village
SJ 927003 *
The company was set up in Park Lane, making gearboxes from 1920 and petrol engines from 1922. Continued success required expansion and the new factory built in the late 1930s on Cannock Road is a tour de force of modernism, steel framed with curtain glass and brick panels, entrance porches and canopies with a hint of Egyptian style. It closed in the late 1970s and is used for warehousing and light industry, unforgivably falling into decay.

WN26 FALLINGS PARK GARDEN SUBURB
Victoria Road
SJ 930004 *
R A S Paget sold an estate for a planned garden suburb and the first houses in a grandiose plan were completed in 1908. The planned chapel and central circular green never materialised and only about fifty houses were built, in short terraces on Victoria Road, The Avenue and Thorneycroft Lane. They have few features to commend them.

WN25 Henry Meadows' engine works

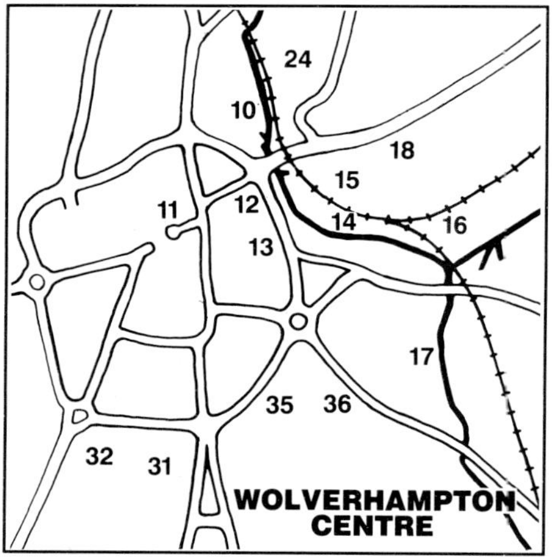

WN27 BUSHBURY HOUSING ESTATE
Low Hill
SJ 923014 area *
A very large geometrical estate developed from 1924 and laid out on a bold plan with radial avenues, crescents and a central circus with shops and library. By early 1928 there were already 1,900 houses, let at rents of 7/6d (37p) per week. Some houses were built c.1930 using Boswell's no-fines cast concrete, but rendering makes them indistinguishable.

WN28 CLYNO MOTOR WORKS
Fourth Avenue, Bushbury
SJ 921009 *
Clyno made cars in Pelham Street, Wolverhampton, from 1911, but in 1925 their excellent sales tempted the company to build a new factory at Bushbury. With a floor space of 4 acres and all new machinery, production began in early 1927; but a cheap model produced to compete with the Morris '8' bankrupted the company and it closed in 1929. An office block fronts large north-light sheds, which are still in use making paper toiletries.

WN31 The Star Motor Company works

WN29 PREFAB ESTATE
Lincoln Green, Bushbury
SJ 918026 *
To assist with emergency housing shortages under the Housing (Temporary Accommodation) Act of 1944, prefabricated single-storey houses were erected in characteristically austere estates, built 1945-46 for an intended ten-year life. This estate retains its original character—the houses themselves, the loop of narrow road, the houses aligned on wide footpaths—almost completely.

WN30 GOODYEAR WORKS
Stafford Road, Oxley
SO 913014 *
Construction began in 1927 and the first British Goodyear tyre was made here in 1928. A greatly expanded site now makes conveyor belting and shoe soles as well as tyres. The blue-painted chimney is a landmark.

WN31 STAR MOTOR COMPANY
Frederick Street
SO 914979 *
Sharratt and Lisle, established 1883 and later renamed the Star Cycle Company, experimented with cars from 1899 and began regular production in 1904. A new works was built here, a symmetrical office building, brick (now rendered) with stone dressings, and fronting north-light assembly sheds. By 1914 'Star' was Britain's sixth largest producer of cars. When Guy took over in 1928 production moved to a new works in Bushbury, ceasing in 1932.

WN32 SUNBEAMLAND WORKS
Paul Street/Jeddo Street
SO 912980 *
John Marston was apprenticed to Edward Perry, tinsmiths and japanners of Jeddo Street in 1851 and in 1871 bought the Works. His first 'Sunbeam' bicycle was built in 1887 and the company and the works expanded rapidly (WN34). The triangular site is full of 3-storey buildings with large windows. The old building in Jeddo Street is part of the old Perry works.

WN33 NIPHON WORKS
Lower Villiers Street
SO 914974 *
Four-storey buildings front the narrow site, and there are three courts of tall narrow workshops behind, all in brick. A classic C19th factory, it was established c.1865 by Robert Stroud & Co. to make tin trunks, tinware and an extensive range of japanned and galvanised ware.

WN34 SUNBEAM MOTORS/VILLIERS
Upper Villiers Street/Marston Road
SO 912973 *
The Villiers Cycle Components Company was established by John Marston in 1898 to make

cycle pedals. The first Sunbeam car was made here in 1899, and in 1905 both companies expanded into new premises. Sunbeam's Moorfield Works in Upper Villiers Street made cars until 1935 and commercial vehicles until the 1960s. Villiers moved into Marston Road to make 2-stroke engines (engines are still made here), and became famous for motorbikes. The latter's office block on Marston Road was demolished in 1982, but cast gates and stone posts covered in symbols remain (**LSII**), together with single and three-storey assembly buildings.

WN35 BAKER'S FOOTWEAR FACTORY
Powlett Street/Cleveland Street
SO 918982 ✻

James Baker established his boot and shoe business in 1850, specialising in *good wearing qualities for the sturdy sons of toil*. The date and the date of extensions in 1890 are recorded over the workpeoples' entrance (under the clock tower) in Powlett Street; this part is single storey, whilst at the other end of the site are 3-storey workshops round a yard. In 1897 341,000 pairs of boots & shoes were made. Now a plumbers's merchants and bankrupt stock store.

WN36 WOLVERHAMPTON WORKS
Cleveland Street
SO 920982 ✻

An ornate 4-storey block with attic dormers, built 1882 for Forder & Co Ltd who in c.1872 won the Society of Arts' prize for an improved Hansom cab; they also championed the introduction of rubber tyres for cabs. Only half the planned works was built; cabs were made until 1911; it is now the showrooms and warehouse of S J Dixon, decorators' merchants.

WN37 JOHN THOMPSON BOILER WORKS
Manor Spring Road, Ettingshall
SO 931964 ✻

A concrete frame building, c.1930 with glass curtain walls dominates the view from Manor Spring Road. Thompsons were established c.1840 at Highfields near Bradley, but moved to Ettingshall in 1870 when it was decided to concentrate on the manufacture of boilers.

WN38 (site of) **BILSTON STEEL WORKS**
Spring Vale
SO 938957 **DEM** ✻

Originating as Springvale Works, the site was acquired in the late 1860s by G. R. Hickman and by 1880 there were five iron-cased furnaces producing 25,000 tons of iron per year. Another company was established in 1882 to develop steelworks using the Thomas-Gilchrist patent. The two companies came together as Alfred Hickman Ltd in 1895, and the company was acquired by Stewarts and Lloyds in 1920. In 1953 the remaining three blast furnaces were replaced by a new blast furnace, 'Elizabeth', but its closure in 1980 brought Black Country ironmaking to an end. The site has been opencast and restored for new uses.

WN39 TRAM DEPOT
Mount Pleasant, Bilston
SO 951967 ✻

The horse tramway routes to Bilston were taken over by the Wolverhampton District Electric Tramways Ltd in 1900, and this site became the main depot. The Midlands Electricity Company transforming station and the tramway offices survive, the latter with a distinctive terracotta symbol.

WN40 (Site of) **BRADLEY IRONWORKS**
Wilkinson Avenue, Bradley
SO 956952 **DEM** ✻

John Wilkinson established his first coke-fired furnace here in 1757-58, which has been called the 'mother furnace'. Soon after he began to use steam power to provide blast, and from here he collaborated with Boulton & Watt to improve the making of steam cylinders. By 1802 there were three furnaces and the forge and rolling mills, with fourteen puddling furnaces, were described as the foremost of England. The site has disappeared without trace, its memorial plaque half a mile adrift (SO 963955) over the Walsall Borough boundary.

WN35 Baker's Boot Manufactory

A name once virtually synonymous with the greater part of the Black Country, the creation of the County of West Midlands in 1974 left a narrow rural strip skirting the west of Wolverhampton and extending down the Smestow Brook valley to Kinver. Trade in iron along the Severn and the potential for water power on the Stour and its tributaries encouraged an early iron industry, later reinforced by Yarranton's improvement of the Stour in 1662-67, and the completion of Brindley's Staffordshire and Worcestershire Canal in 1772. In the early twentieth century Kinver enjoyed a reputation as a week-end recreation centre for Black Country folk.

SS1 AWBRIDGE LOCK

Lower Penn

SO 860949 **SC LSII CA** ✻

Here the tail bridge carries a road and has parapets carried on nine brick pillars. Boaters cross the lock on a cast iron bracketed footbridge split to allow towropes to pass. Adjacent are a modernised lock cottage and a fine example of Brindley's circular overflow weirs.

SS2 THE BRATCH LOCKS

Wombourn

SO 867938 **LSII CA** ✻

Thought to have been built as a staircase triple, the three chambers were rebuilt at an unknown date with minute pounds between them, connecting via culverts with side pounds laid out on the hillside to the west. Though boats cannot pass, this arrangement is less wasteful of water. Next to the upper chamber's roving tail bridge is a small octagonal tollhouse. The towpath passes under a road bridge and there are narrow steps giving access to boats below the bottom lock.

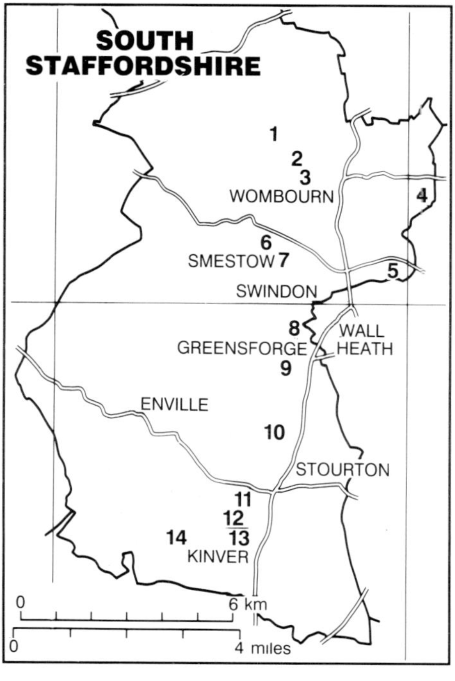

SS3 THE BRATCH PUMPING STATION

Wombourn

SO 869937 **LSII** ✻

A gothic extravaganza in brick with corner pinnacles, by Baldwin Latham for the Bilston UDC Waterworks Company. The James Watt & Co triple expansion engines were completed by Thornewill and Wareham of Burton after the bankruptcy of the designers. Pumping commenced in 1895. The steam plant was replaced by submersible pumps in 1960, but has been retained by the South Staffs Water Board and latterly by Severn Trent.

SS3 The Bratch water pumping station

SS9 Coal drops ai Ashwood Basin in the 1940s

SS4 (Site of) **BAGGERIDGE COLLIERY**
Fir Street, Gospel End
SO 898931 ✱
The mine was sunk in 1912 to reach the thick coal at a depth of 1680ft west of the boundary faults. It was the last Black Country pit to close, in 1968. Only the bases of the two shafts survive, in a landscaped country park, but the brickworks still operates. The track of the colliery railway, a branch of the Earl of Dudley's private Pensnett Railway, can be traced.

SS5 THE GLYNNE ARMS
Himley
SO 897908 ❑
Known locally as the Crooked House, the steep angles result from mining subsidence. Recent extensions have spoiled the character of this former C19th farmhouse.

SS6 SMESTOW WATER MILL
Smestow
SO 856916 LSII ✱
Early C19th watermill, 2 and 3-storey in brick, with machinery of 1839, and an iron breast-shot wheel under a shed at the rear.

SS7 BOTTERHAM LOCKS
Swindon
SO 860913 **CA** ✱
Reputedly Brindley's first use, c.1770 of the staircase lock principle, with a fall of 20ft in two chambers sharing three pairs of gates. The adjacent lock cottage has been modernised, losing a bay window in the process.

SS8 KINGSWINFORD (SHUT END) RAILWAY
Swindon Road, Wall Heath
SO 871894 ✱
The embankment and abutments of the bridge over Swindon Road mark the railway which was completed in 1829 by John Rastrick for James Foster to carry coal and iron from the Shut End estate to the Staffordshire and Worcestershire Canal at Ashwood Basin (SS8). The railway was opened amid great celebrations with Rastrick's locomotive *Agenoria* (now in The Science Museum, London) on June 2nd 1829.

SS9 ASHWOOD BASIN
Greensforge
SO 866884 **CA** ■
600 metre long basin from the Staffs and Worcs Canal built in conjunction with the Kingswinford Railway, opened June 1829. Coal traffic ceased in October 1953 when canal carrying of Baggeridge coal to Stourport Power Station ceased. Now a marina, but fragments of the coaling stages and an office building survive. A minor road crosses the basin by an eleven-arched, weight-restricted bridge.

SS10 GOTHERSLEY ROUND HOUSE
Stourton
SO 863867 **CA** ✱
The ruins of a keeper's cottage built c.1805 for the wharf serving the Gothersley Ironworks on the west side of the canal. The works was flourishing in 1830, with forges and mills, but closed c.1880.

SS11 THE HYDE TRAM DEPOT
Kinver
SO 852844 ■
A four-road tram depot in the middle of a wood for the Kinver Light Railway which opened in 1901. It was active in the summer season, and stored open cars during winter. Closed in 1930, the corrugated iron building has gone but the two inspection pits can still be found.

SS12 THE HYDE IRONWORKS
Kinver
SO 846838 **CA** ✱
A canalside cottage and fragments of a

SS12 Bolton and Lee's Hyde iron works

spillway remain from the ironworks founded by Richard Foley c.1628 and reputed to be the site of the first slitting mill in Britain. The works was operated by Bolton and Lee in the 1870s, with twenty puddling furnaces and two Siemens open hearth steel furnaces, but it closed soon after 1880.

SS13 KINVER TRAM TERMINUS

Kinver

SO 848834 ❑

The Kinver Light Railway operated electric tramcars from 1901 to 1930, bringing thousands of Black Country folk on day trips to this attractive village in the narrow Smestow valley. The terminus was a spartan affair, with corrugated iron waiting room, ticket office and toilets. The perimeter fencing is still in place.

SS14 ROCK HOUSES

Kinver Edge

SO 835836 ❑

In the Severn valley rooms and dwellings hewn from the solid red sandstone were not uncommon. Here at Holy Austin Rock are the remains of houses on three levels, including a terrace of three, the last of which was inhabited until c.1950. Evidence of former gardens and service pipes can be found. The large room below was a well-known tea-room in the 1920s. Recently some rooms have been cut away because of the danger from erosion by visitors.

SS13 A tram at Kinver terminus

As used here the term 'Mid-Severn Valley' conforms to no recognisable geographical boundaries, but is taken for the purposes of this guide to be those parts of Shropshire and Worcestershire between and including the immediate valleys of the Severn (from Bridgnorth to Stourport) and Stour. Predominantly rural and agricultural, the influences of two great waterway arteries have left linear patterns of industrial heritage between the towns.

On the Severn itself, a free river unencumbered by tolls from the C13th, the towns of Bewdley and Bridgnorth have both been important crossing points and river ports. The eighteenth century houses of Bewdley's Severnside reflect the former dominance of the river as a trade artery. Bridgnorth became a small industrial town in its own right with a famous foundry and an outlier of the carpet-weaving industry, both now demolished. The Severn itself is too unpredictable to provide water power, but its entrenched tributaries provided sites for industry availing itself of raw materials passing along the river between the Coalbrookdale district and the sea. The river has cut down towards the Coal Measures, and there were productive mines at Highley and Alveley.

Stourport is also on the Severn, but its significance relates to the junction of the Staffordshire and Worcestershire Canal with the river. The canal was completed in 1772 and the basins at Stourport became important for the transfer of all kinds of goods from the narrow canal system to the wide Severn trows. Chief amongst these were the materials and products of the iron industry; the already established (in 1772) trade in pig iron from the Forest of Dean and South Wales to the Stour Valley forges and slitting mills; the finished rods and nails of the rolling mills and domestic workshops, and later the whole range of iron products from the Black Country. Bricks, especially the Staffordshire Blues and the Stourbridge firebricks in all their varieties, came down the canal in huge quantities, and the coal traffic survived until the 1950s.

Kidderminster, some three miles upstream the Stour valley from its confluence with the Severn, is the largest town in this district. Whilst it owes some of its economic prosperity to the canal, it is more in debt to a long-established woollen and silk weaving industry which flourished from the C16th and was already in decline when the canal arrived. But the weaving of carpets had already been tried, and from the end of the eighteenth into the early nineteenth centuries the new industry swamped the old; in 1799 Nash estimated. that there were 250 carpet looms in the town as against 1700 worsted and silk looms, but by 1807 there were 1,000 carpet looms and only 700 worsted and silk looms. Real success came with the introduction of the powered carpet loom from 1852, and the late nineteenth century saw the development of enormous weaving sheds in a prosperity which turned parts of the town into a pastiche of West Yorkshire. The prosperity continued during most of the twentieth century, only to burst in recent years.

MS1 (site of) **HAZELDINE'S FOUNDRY**
off Mill Street, Bridgnorth
SO 721928 *
Dating from c.1795, the foundry lay behind Mill Street towards the river, and became famous as the maker of Trevithick's high-pressure steam engine. John Urpeth Rastrick was a partner from 1803 to 1816 and was probably involved in the building of Trevithick's London locomotive of 1808. There is a commemorative plaque on the clock tower at the east end of the bridge; none of the industrial buildings survive.

MS2 CASTLE HILL CLIFF RAILWAY
Bridgnorth
SO 718929 ❑
The only funicular railway in inland Britain, connecting High Town with Low Town near the river bridge. It was opened in 1892 as a water balance with a 2,000 gallon tank beneath each car, and converted to electric winding in 1944.

MS3 ST MARY & ST MICHAEL
Bridgnorth
SO 717928 **LSII** ❑
Built 1796/97, a fine example of a church designed by Telford when he was County Surveyor for Shropshire.

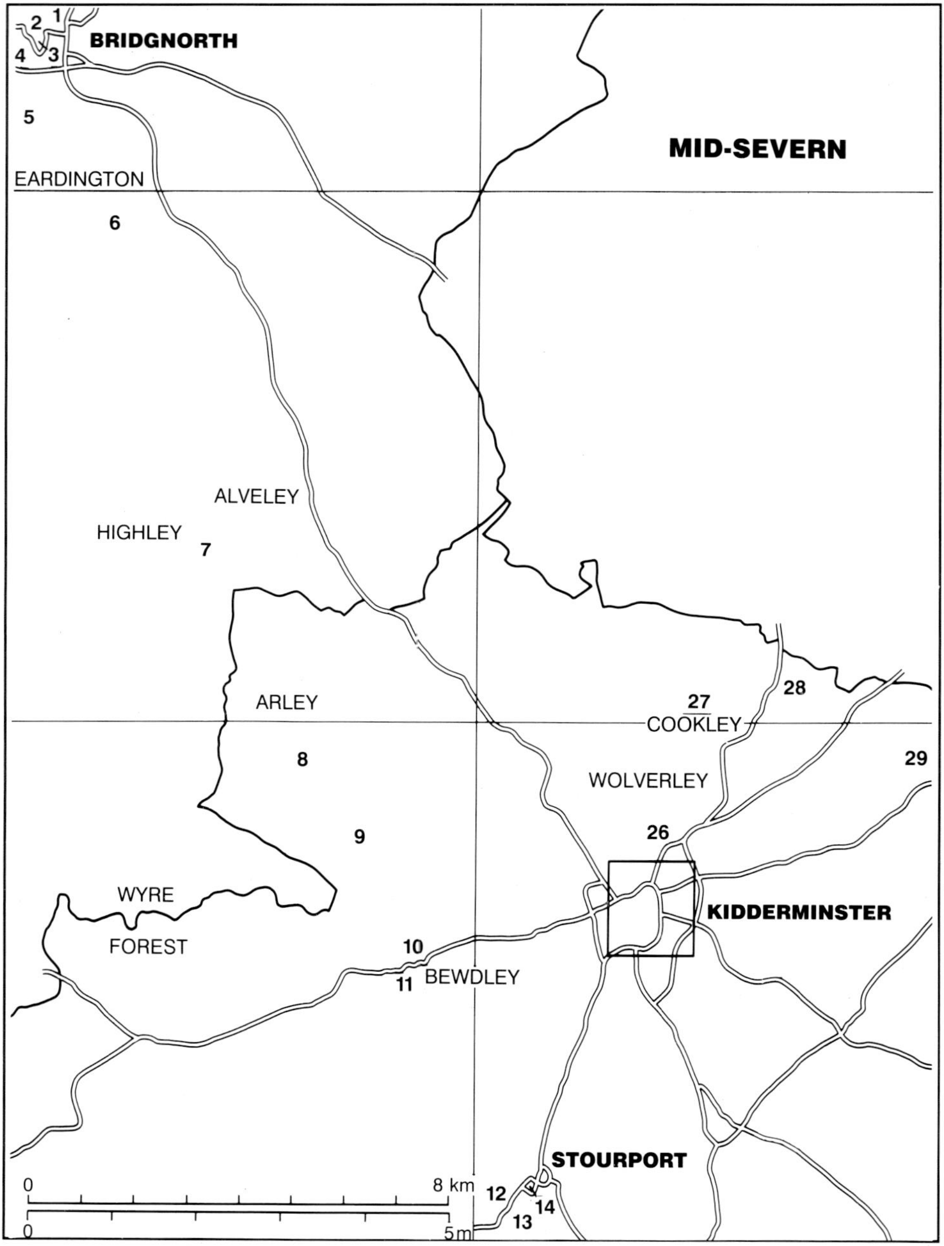

MS4 RAILWAY STATION

Bridgnorth

SO 715926 ❑

The GWR's Severn Valley line opened in 1862 and closed in 1963. Demolition had reached as far south as Bridgnorth when it was halted by a strong preservation group, and the station survives complete as the northern terminus of the present Severn Valley Railway. Many items have been collected from the former GWR and other railways; the main engine workshops have grown around the former goods shed. There are plans to rebuild the high level footbridge which once linked the station to High Town.

MS2 Car at head of the cliff railway, Bridgnorth

MS5 DANIEL'S MILL

off Eardington Road, Bridgnorth

SO 718917 **LSII** ❑

A fine water powered corn mill nestling below the railway viaduct, with a 38ft diameter cast iron wheel, now operating mid-breast and driving three pairs of stones through a layshaft. The mill worked into the 1950s and is again producing flour. Open to visitors (admission charge).

MS5 Daniel's Mill, Bridgnorth

MS6 EARDINGTON FORGES

SO 724897 and 733895 ✳

Two associated works approximately 2•5 miles S of Bridgnorth. The Upper Forge on the Mor Brook dates from medieval times, and was enlarged in 1778. The Lower Forge was built in 1782, together with a canal (part in tunnel) linking it with the Upper Forge and bringing water to power the waterwheels. The works were acquired by John Bradley & Co in 1839 and closed in 1869. The striking Upper Forge weir in dense private woodland and the canal (now part of a fish farm) remain, as do workers' cottages, various building fragments and a chimney at the Lower Forge.

MS7 HIGHLEY & ALVELEY COLLIERIES

SO 746829 and 754840 ■

The Wyre Forest coalfield extended from Bridgnorth to Abberley and was worked in many small pits. The Highley Mining Company worked the Brooch seam at Highley from 1874 to the 1930s when a new shaft was sunk on the east bank of the Severn at Alveley. This worked until 1969, the coal being carried by aerial ropeway to a coal preparation plant and railway sidings. The site has been landscaped, but the private bridge over the river and the sidings site on the SVR remain.

MS8 VICTORIA BRIDGE

nr Arley

SO 766793 **LSII★** ✳

Designed by John Fowler, cast by the Coalbrookdale Company and completed June 1861, the largest cast iron arch bridge of its time. Four ribs each consisting of nine sections, with a span of 200ft and a rise of 20ft, carry the SVR across the Severn.

MS9 CHALET SITES

north of Bewdley

SO 782768 ■

All along the Severn valley are long-established chalet and caravan sites, which once contained an amazing variety of old showman's caravans, buses, and railway coaches. Few now remain, but the idiosyncrasies of these summer bolt-holes from the midlands towns are well seen from the Severn Valley Railway.

MS10 BEWDLEY BRIDGE

SO 787754 **LSI** ❑

The old bridge was destroyed in the great Severn floods of 1795 and the present elegant five-arched stone structure was designed by Telford in Arley stone, and completed in 1801 at a cost of £9,300. Bewdley was an important river centre, and the eighteenth century sandstone wharves along Severnside can still be seen to the south of the bridge. There were important boat-building yards to the north.

MS12 Stourport Bridge

MS11 BEWDLEY MUSEUM
Load Street, Bewdley
SO 786753 ❑
A small museum occupying The Shambles, and including a small brass foundry and a former ropeworks, with interesting displays relating to industries of the town (including coracle-making) and the trades of nearby Wyre Forest.

MS12 RIVER BRIDGE
Stourport
SO 808710 **LSII** ❑
A fine cast iron bridge, with five ribs each of five segments, stayed by wrought iron bars keyed into sockets. The date 1870 and *S B T* is cast on shields in the spandrels, but the maker's name is not recorded. The bridge is approached by a long series of brick flood relief arches.

MS13 CANAL BASINS
Stourport
SO 810711 **LSII** ❑
Brindley's Staffordshire and Worcestershire Canal originally joined the Severn via a canal basin (Middle), accessible from the river through two wide locks without fixed bridges to permit masted trows to enter. Building began c.1768, the Lower basin and two sets of closely spaced two-rise narrow locks (**LSII**) were opened in 1781 and a clock was added to the central 'Clock Warehouse' (**LSII**) in 1812. There are many interesting canal-related features; the Tontine Hotel (**LSII**) was built by the Canal Company for the passenger trade, and a nice group of cottages and a pub face the river.

MS13 Middle Basin and Clock Warehouse, Stourport

MS14 LOCK AND TOLL COTTAGE
York Street, Bewdley
SO 812712 **LSII** ❑
The first lock on the Staffs and Worcestershire Canal's long climb up the Stour and Smestow valleys, with angled balance beams on the lower gates to avoid fouling the tail bridge. The tiny toll office bears the date 1853, and the lock cottage, now a shop, is dated 1854.

MS15 WATERWORKS
Green Road, Kidderminster
SO 831759 ✱
A small pumping station, brick with cream terracotta dressings, bearing the legend *Kidderminster Water Works 1905*. An earlier engine house, in yellow brick with a high parapet hiding the pitched roof, is now part of the Council Depot across the road.

MS16 HOUSES
Park Lane, Kidderminster
SO 828760 ✱
A row of twelve large houses in two groups, supposedly built for carpet manufacturers, in red and yellow brick with half timber effect

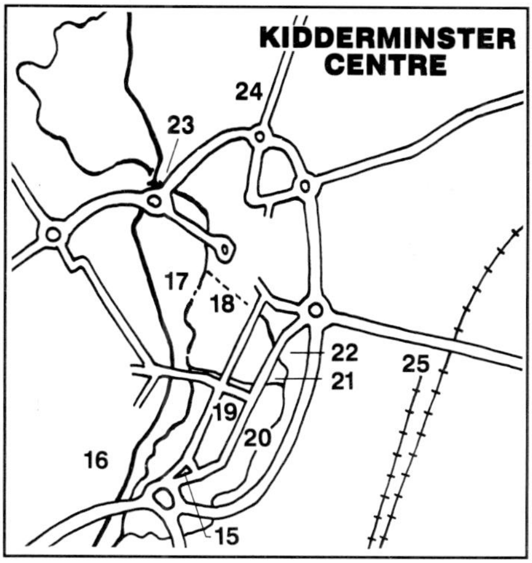

towers which are reputed to lack stairs and are therefore inaccessible from inside.

MS17 BRINTONS CARPET FACTORY

The Sling, Kidderminster

SO 831765 ✻

Samuel Brinton was making Brussels carpets in Kidderminster c.1770, and the company bought other premises to develop what is now a huge and complex site. Slingfield Spinning Mill (**LSII**) had been built c.1864 for George Lea, 4 storeys in polychrome brick with pointed window heads in the local style, an attached engine house and detached boiler house and chimney with blind lancets (**LSII**), and is the most impressive building, sadly underused. Another spinning mill, many huge weaving sheds and a complex range of offices with various dates to the east of the site reflect a continuous expansion, and the company has modern buildings on Stourport Road. Various companies were swallowed up, and the company amalgamated with Crossley's in 1953.

MS16 Carpet manufacturers' houses, Kidderminster

MS18 SCHOOL OF SCIENCE & ART

Market Street, Kidderminster

SO 832764 ✻

A 'triple institute of literature, science and art', erected and opened in three stages, the School of Art in 1879, School of Science in 1887 and the Library in 1894. Art was specifically to serve the ends of good carpet design, and the science gave technical training for the industry. Designed by J H Gethin and built of Stourbridge firebrick with decorative terracotta (especially the mullion shafts), the building is empty and its future uncertain.

MS19 PADDINGTON HOUSE

New Road, Kidderminster

SO 832762 ✻

This former carpet factory has a fine 3-storey office block with tower, in brick with a variety of window styles. Further down the road are large single-storey loom shops with north lights. The mill was begun by G M Whittall & Co in 1868 and the office dates from 1877. Later it belonged to the Carpet Manufacturing Company, and is now occupied by a shoe supply company.

MS20 VICTORIA CARPET WORKS

Green Street, Kidderminster

SO 833763 ✻

The company moved here from Kirkaldy in 1899 to make tapestry and velvet pile carpets, taking over the factory of William Green & Sons which is the pedimented building. Extensions were added on both sides, and a c.1930s office continues the tradition of blue brick.

MS21 CHLIDEMA CARPET WORKS

Green Street, Kidderminster

SO 834762 ✻

A plain office building fronting single-storey weaving sheds. The company was established in 1887 to exploit the invention of a Jacquard control system which allowed the weaving of patterned carpet squares, which were previously made by cutting and sewing the corners.

MS22 WOODWARD-GROSVENOR CARPETS

Green Street, Kidderminster

SO 834763 ✻

The company leased in 1864 and later purchased the Stour Vale Mills built by the Earl of Dudley to help the ailing hand loom industry by providing room and power for power carpet looms. The handsome office building, red brick with yellow brick dressings, round head windows and stone pediments, has been extended and hides large single-storey loom shops.

MS22 Woodward-Grosvenor Carpet factory

MS23 CANAL WHARF

off St Mary's Ringway, Kidderminster

SO 829769 ✳

The Staffordshire and Worcestershire Canal crosses the Stour on a three-arch aqueduct and immediately falls through a lock to pass under the ring road. Just above there was a short canal arm with wharves and warehouses, all now 'tidied away', but a wharfing crane survives.

MS23 Canal wharf by St Mary's, Kidderminster

MS24 TOMKINSONS CARPET WORKS

Churchfields, Kidderminster

SO 832772 ✳

A two-storey mill dated 1902 and flanked by single-storey weaving sheds, all in red brick with blue dressings, one gable dated 1932. Established in 1867 to make rugs on hand looms, looms were brought from America to make Axminster and chenille.

MS25 RAILWAY STATION

Comberton Hill, Kidderminster

SO 828763 ❑

The elaborate GWR half-timbered style station has been demolished, but the Severn Valley Railway Company's new terminus station is modelled on the Ross-on-Wye buildings. The former goods shed is now the SVR carriage repair shop.

MS26 STOUR VALE MILLS

off Springfield Lane, Kidderminster

SO 824778 ✳

A solitary factory chimney standing in a pond marks the site of the Broadwaters Iron and Tinplate Works. There are ponds and sluices further up the valley (SO 842780 and 846779). Just downstream were Richard Thomas & Baldwin's Stour Vale Works, founded in 1867. In 1935 they introduced the cold-rolling of steel to Britain.

MS27 COOKLEY IRONWORKS

Cookley

SO 841806 ✳

The works was founded c.1650 by John Knight, and in 1860 a patent process for tinplating was introduced. Cookley 'K' tinplate was renowned, but the works closed in 1887. In 1904 the Chaddesley Corbett Manufacturing Co. began making cart and artillery wheels, and pressed wheels are still made for the motor trade. The canal tunnels deep under Bridge Street.

MS28 SLEEPY MILL

off A449, Caunsall

SO 855806 ■

A small rural water mill dated 1665 with a composite wheel in semi-derelict condition, in a private garden but visible from the road.

MS29 CHURCHILL FORGE

Churchill

SO 883796 **SC LSII** ❑ (Occasionally)

The site has exploited water power since the C13th and was a blade mill by the C16th. A brick-faced dam holds back a large pool, below which are two waterwheels; one drove two tilt hammers under which scythes, shovels and other edge tools were forged. Later a range of forged ladles was made for foundries. The forge operated until 1970, and is currently being restored for public access.

England's second city breaks all the rules of urban location. Its hilltop and river crossing are insignificant, it stands on no major routeway, and it lies far from the coast. Yet as early as 1538 Leland was shocked by the noise of the smiths whose premises lined the streets, encouraged by a free market, freedom from guild restrictions and the ready supply of Black Country coal. A spirit of independence bred many industries—cloth-making, leather trades, lorinery and cutlery. In the seventeenth century gunmaking arrived, and the metal trades grew as cloth and leather declined. The first patent for button making dates from 1631, and buckle making in steel and other metals—the 'toy' trade—was well established by the early eighteenth century.

It was the eighteenth century which saw Birmingham's development as 'the cradle of invention', with the Quakers Sampson Lloyd and John Taylor establishing a bank, and with the ascendancy of Matthew Boulton, perhaps the greatest of all industrial entrepreneurs. Born in 1728, Boulton took over his father's button business in 1759, and commissioned Samuel Wyatt to build the Soho Manufactory, opened in 1762. Soon over 1,000 operatives worked there, stamping, pressing, piercing, casting and machining innumerable designs in all kinds of metals. Of the many innovations from Soho the most famous was the Watt steam engine from 1776, when the Boulton & Watt partnership began to sell 'what all the world wanted—power!' The same period saw the promotion of the canal system which broke Birmingham's isolation from the sea, and the flowering of the Lunar Society whose members contributed to the further development of free thought and new ideas.

Subsequent developments have confirmed Birmingham's centrality, with railway companies fighting for its trade in the nineteenth century and the motorways focusing there in recent years. The city's political leaders played a prominent role in national reform, as well as fostering a full range of civic and cultural institutions at home. Industrial diversity has also remained the city's hallmark, both in the range of production and the size of units. The famous jewellery and gun quarters still house individual craftsmen in tiny workshops, each contributing their particular skill to the manufacture of the finished product. The same principle holds at the other end of the scale, in the huge works where motor vehicles are put together on assembly lines from components made in hundreds of smaller factories throughout the region.

The volume and variety of industry leaves a heritage which is not always respected, perhaps because there is so much of it. Birmingham deserves a volume to itself, and this guide presents only a small sample of the city's industrial past.

BM1 PERRY BARR LOCKS

Perry Park

SP 058927 to 076923 ❑

Seven of the Tame Valley Canal's thirteen locks, opened 1844, are grouped in a straight flight here. The canal bypassed the congestion of the city centre, and was engineered with huge cuttings and embankments.

BM2 ASTON MANOR TRAM DEPOT

Witton Lane

SP 078904 ❑ (occasionally)

A long shed with four entrances and parallel tracks, built by the Birmingham and Aston Tramways Co. for the use of steam trams and opened in December 1882. It was acquired by Birmingham Corporation in 1904 and operated electric trams until 1950. It was then a car showroom, but is again owned by the city housing a collection of historic road vehicles.

BM3 ELECTRIC AVENUE

Witton

SP 086904 ❑

Named from the various works of the General Electric Company, which date from 1900 and came to cover 150 acres. The two-storey office block, visible from the gate, is Egyptian in style, rendered with an imposing Portland stone entrance. Behind is an enormous erecting shed, very obvious from the elevated M6 motorway. The west side of the avenue developed as housing for the workforce at GEC and the neighbouring Mond Nickel Co works.

BM4 SPAGHETTI JUNCTION
M6 Motorway, Aston
SP 083904 ❑
Britain's first complex motorway intersection towers on concrete columns over the River Tame and Salford canal junction. Built 1968-1971.

BM5 TERRACOTTA BUILDINGS
Lichfield Road, Aston
SP 098896 ❑
Birmingham has many examples of commercial premises incorporating terracotta: here the Church Tavern, brown glaze and cream; the Swan and Mitre, 1898 in flamboyant red; and the Britannia, brown glaze and cream with a terracotta Britannia on the parapet, are worth notice. The cast iron clock at Aston Cross (SP 080889, **LSII**) was made by the Sun Foundry, Glasgow, in 1891.

BM6 WOLSELEY WORKS
Drews Lane, Ward End
SP 112892 ✻
A factory and workers' cottages were built here in the 1890s, acquired by Vickers in 1899, and much expanded to make and fill shells during the First War. Wolseley cars were then assembled here until Morris bought the company in 1926; it then became a components plant. By 1970 Drews Lane claimed to have the largest machine shop in Europe. Latterly the Freight-rover range has been assembled here; now part of Leyland Daf. A long symmetrical 2-storey office block, 1915, (brick, stone bands and dressings) fronts the assembly buildings.

BM7 FORT DUNLOP
Dunlop Way, Bromford
SP 129903 ✻
An enormous 8-storey rectangular warehouse block in bright red brick with square turrets and a smaller 4-storey block in the same style are the dominant features of this huge site. Nicknamed *Tyre Town*, it was established in 1916 to manufacture solid rubber tyres, and had its own internal rail system, power station and recreation facilities. In the 1950s 10,000 people were employed in its 3 million sqft. Dunlop still make tyres and other products here, but the large block is empty and seeking new uses.

BM8 (site of) **SOHO MANUFACTORY**
Factory Road, Handsworth
SP 051890 **DEM** ✻
There are no remains of Matthew Boulton's famous 'Manufactory' established in 1762 for the manufacture of buckles, buttons and other small metal goods. Factory Road recalls the site which was cleared in 1848, and the railway sidings are built on the site of the former Soho Pool from which water was returned above the Works by steam engine. Nearby Soho House, built 1789 by Samuel Wyatt for Boulton, is being restored. Boulton and Watt are both buried and commemorated in St Michael's Church.

BM9 SOHO, ICKNEILD PORT AND OOZELLS STREET CANAL LOOPS
Ladywood
SP 049878, 048872 and 057867 ❑
Brindley's Birmingham Canal opened in 1772 followed a sinuous course, the 'crooked ditch'

BM7 Fort Dunlop

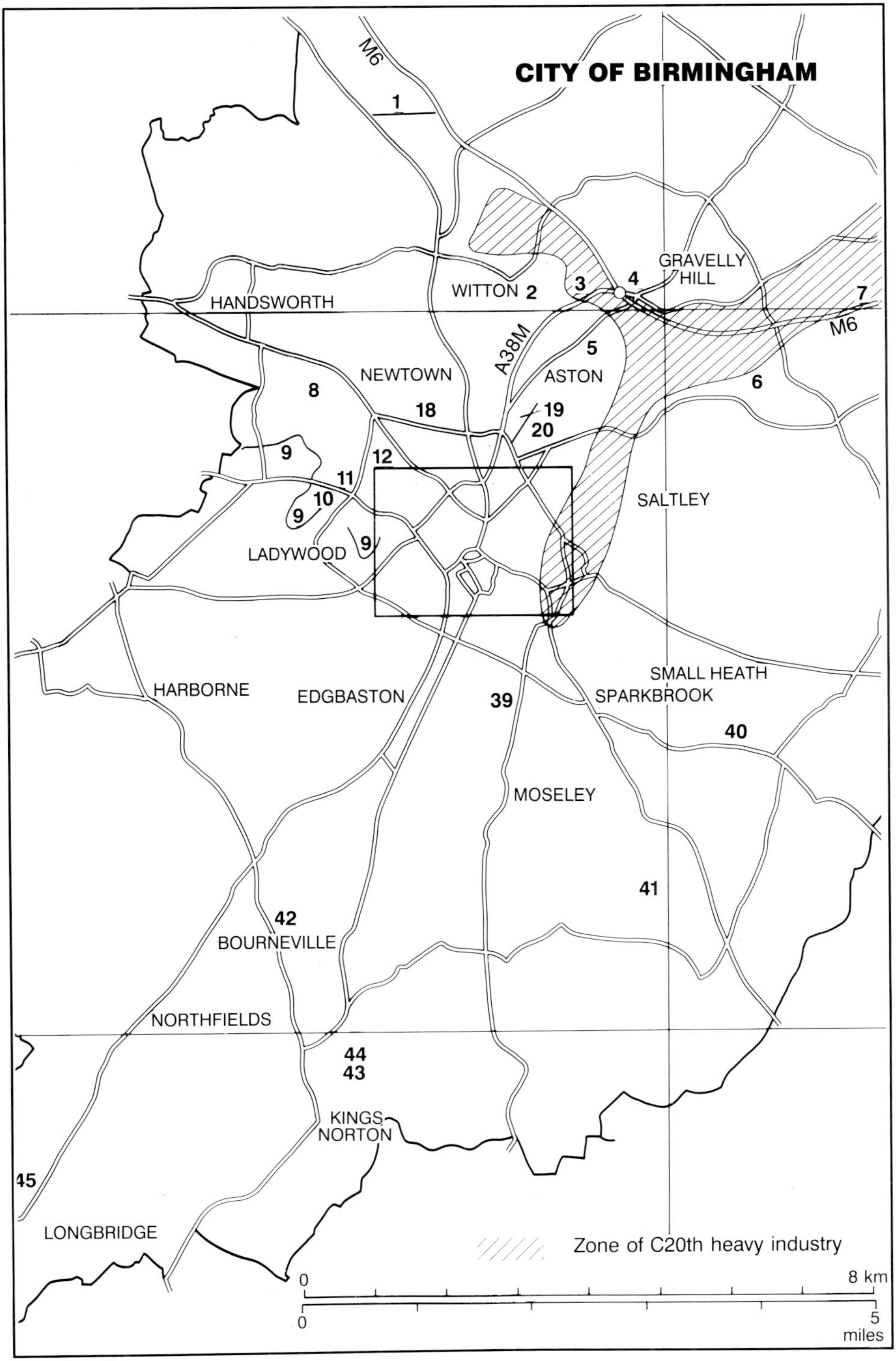
CITY OF BIRMINGHAM
M6
1
WITTON 2
3
4
GRAVELLY HILL
7
M6
HANDSWORTH
A38M
5
ASTON
NEWTOWN
6
8
18
19
20
9
12
11
10
9
SALTLEY
9
LADYWOOD
SMALL HEATH
HARBORNE
EDGBASTON
39
SPARKBROOK
40
MOSELEY
41
42
BOURNEVILLE
NORTHFIELDS
44
43
KINGS NORTON
45
LONGBRIDGE
Zone of C20th heavy industry
0
8 km
0
5 miles

which was largely bypassed by Telford's 'New Line', engineered on the grand scale and completed in 1827. The loops, with striking cast iron roving bridges at the junctions, remained navigable to provide access to the many works and wharves along them.

BM10 BELLIS & MORCOM

Icknield Square, Ladywood

SP 050873 ✱

Included to exemplify the city's heavy engineering trade, the works covers a large area of the Icknield Canal Loop. The firm was established in 1861, introduced its famous enclosed vertical steam engines in 1891, and still makes compressors. Nearby in Ledsham Street Bellis' earlier 3-storey Ledsham Works survives (SP 054868).

BM11 PUBLIC LIBRARY

Spring Hill

SP 055874 **LSII★** ❑

A superb example of Birmingham civic building, designed by Chamberlain & Martin and completed in 1893. The exterior is red terracotta with flamboyant decoration incorporating the usual City arms and motto; inside are marble columns and gothic arches.

BM12 THE BIRMINGHAM MINT

Icknield Street

SP 057878 **LSII** ✱

Matthew Boulton set up a mint at Soho in 1796 which produced coinage until 1850. Some presses were sold to Ralph Heaton who moved his Birmingham Mint, established 1829, to this site in 1860. A 2-storey office with coat of arms over the door fronts later buildings.

BM13 THE JEWELLERY QUARTER

Great Hampton Street, Warstones Lane etc

SP 063876 (area) many: **LSII** ❑ ✱

The area, developed continuously from the late eighteenth century, contains hundreds of interesting buildings; former houses with rear workshops stand next to purpose-built works large and small. A very few examples are: **Victoria Works**, Frederick Street (SP 062874, **LSII**), multi-floored workshops in a walled court, built 1838-45 for Joseph Gillott, steel pen maker. The bust of Queen Victoria was added in 1887. Recently refurbished as studios and 'warehouse-style apartments'.

Argent Works, Frederick Street (SP 061874, **LSII★**), a riot of Italianate style in polychrome brick, once Gallenkamp & Co. and recently restored for offices. **Unity Works**, Vittoria Street (SP 062875, **LSII**), built c.1865 for Henry Jenkins, 'stampers, piercers, spinners and pressers'.

Chamberlain Clock, Vyse Street/Warstones Lane (SP 061877, **LSII**), a cast iron memorial of Joseph Chamberlain's visit to South Africa in 1903. **Crowngate House**, Gt Hampton Street; a very large 1920s building, striped in brick and cream terracotta. Nearby is the smaller **Pelican Works** (**LSII**), a large stone bird on its parapet.

BM14 MUSEUM OF SCIENCE AND INDUSTRY

Newhall Street

SP 064873 ❑

Elkington's, who developed electro-plating for silver and gilt in 1836, expanded onto this site in the 1840s. The buildings now contain

BM14 Roving bridge, Aston top lock

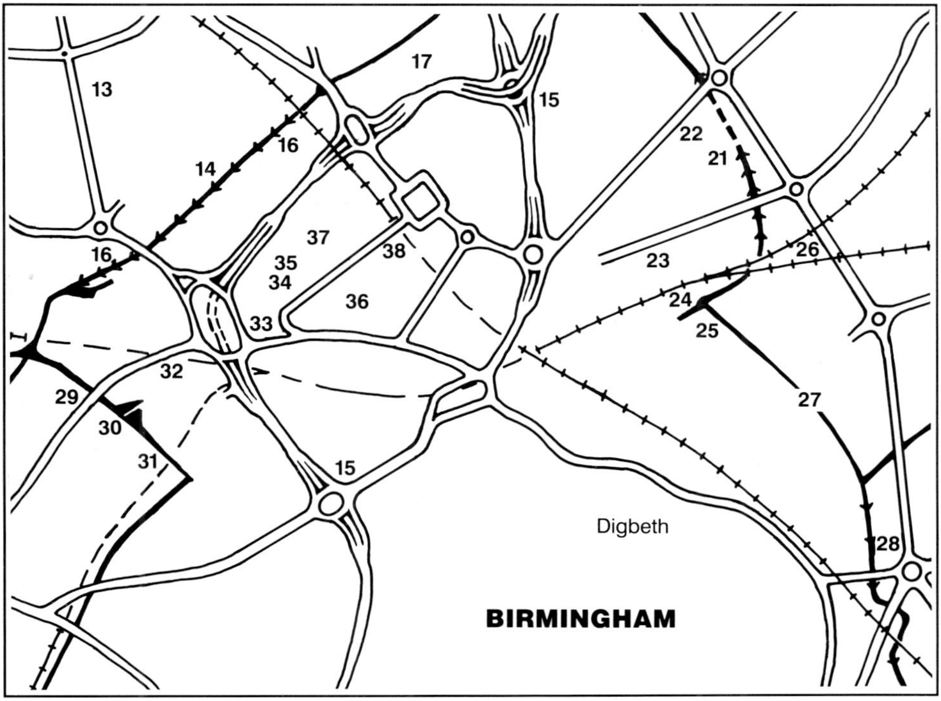

important collections relating to the city's diverse industrial history. The Smethwick engine of 1779, by Boulton & Watt (SA31), is steamed regularly.

BM15 QUEENSWAY

(Inner Ring Road)

SP 068864, 074876 ✳

This tight circle round the city centre, burrowing under radial roads and the library, was planned in the 1960s as a ground-level dual carriageway to restrict public transport; *essential traffic will be free to use the city centre as it wishes, and shoppers will have greater freedom of movement with the removal of buses*.

BM16 FARMERS BRIDGE LOCKS

off Summer Row

SP 061870 to 069876 ❑

Built 1786-9 by the amalgamated Birmingham and Birmingham and Fazeley Canal Company, thirteen locks with a fall of 81ft now burrow under modern buildings. At the top, the much shortened Newhall Branch forms a basin, Brindley Wharf, restored in the 1960s with two wooden cranes. Canalside features abound.

BM17 GUN QUARTER

Loveday Street/Bath Street.

SP 072877 ❑ ✳

In Bath Street are two late C19th 2-storey workshops, one still making guns, next to the Gunmakers Arms (**LSII**). Nearby, New Buildings, 63 Price Street, still contains 10 gun-parts makers, including a gunbarrel filer, stockmaker, gun engraver, and a gun action hardener.

BM18 JOSEPH LUCAS LTD

Great King Street, Newtown

SP 064887 ✳

Established in 1872 to make ship and cycle lamps, the company built new premises here from 1897. Two very large symmetrical brick buildings either side of the now closed-off street are linked by a bridge.

BM19 GRAZEBROOK ENGINE

Dartmouth Circus

SP 077883 ❑

A beam blowing engine designed by Boulton, Watt & Co and built at Deepfields, Coseley, in 1817 for Grazebrook's Netherton Ironworks. It worked until 1912 and again in 1939-44; when the furnaces closed in 1952 the engine was presented to Birmingham and erected on the traffic island in 1971.

BM20 ASTON LOCKS

off Mill Street/Dartmouth Middleway

SP 077881 to 087892 **LSII** ❑

Below Farmers Bridge locks the Birmingham & Fazeley falls through another eight locks from Aston Junction. The junction is spanned by a fine cast roving bridge made by the Horseley Ironworks, Staffordshire, in 1828, and the top lock has, unusually, a brick tail bridge.

BM19 The Grazebrook engine

BM21 ASHTED LOCKS AND TUNNEL

off Curzon Street

SP 079877 to 082872 ❑

The short Ashted Tunnel follows immediately from the top lock, and is itself followed by five more locks which take the Digbeth Branch under the railways to Digbeth Basin and a junction with the Warwick & Birmingham Canal.

BM22 CWS WORKS

Belmont Row, Nechells Green

SP 079875 ✻

A prominent 3-storey works building dated 1899 in brick with cream terracotta, with offices at one end and a 'Workmen and Goods' entrance at the other.

BM23 CURZON STREET STATION

Curzon Street

SP 078871 **LSI** ✻

A solid classical structure by Philip Hardwick to mark the northern end of the London and Birmingham Railway, the counterpart to the lamented Euston Arch. A square ashlar building with Ionic columned portico, it was opened in June 1838 and superseded by New Street station in 1854. It was used by excursion trains until 1893 and then as a goods station until 1968. Bought and restored by the City Council, it houses the offices of The Prince's Trust.

BM24 GUN BARREL PROOF HOUSE

Banbury Street

SP 079869 **LSII** ✻

The Birmingham gun trade dates from the 1690s, but expanded greatly during the Napoleonic Wars. The Proof House was built in 1813 by John Horton, for the testing of gun barrels

BM23 London & Birmingham Railway, Curzon Street Station

with charges 30% above their stated limits. The elegant brick building with its once central ornamented entrance is now overshadowed by railway viaducts.

BM24 Gun Barrel Proof House

BM25 WARWICK BAR
off Fazeley Street
SP 081869 ❑
The Warwick & Birmingham made a junction with the Birmingham Canal's Digbeth Branch (1799) through a stop lock with two sets of single gates so as to cope with high water level either side. There is a nice single-storey warehouse (**LSII**) and nearby a 3-storey warehouse, 'The Bond', in red and blue-striped brick with a large wooden lucam.

BM26 RAILWAY VIADUCTS
Lawley Street/Great Barr Street
SP 082872 (area) and SP 077866 ❋
The London and Birmingham, Grand Junction, Midland and Great Western Railways all approach the city on viaducts across the valley of the River Rea. The most interesting is the former Grand Junction line, in stone with a ramped upper tier added in blue brick for access to New Street. The construction of Duddeston Viaduct, intended to link the GWR to Curzon Street, was halted c.1850 when relations between the GWR and LNWR turned sour. It was never finished and parts have been demolished.

BM27 CANAL BRIDGE
Great Barr Street
SP 077866 **LSII** ❑
Bridge 95 on the Warwick & Birmingham Canal is formed of cast arched plates between cast spandrels with parapets of cast plates rivetted together. Nearby, nestling against a pier of Duddleston Viaduct (abandoned c.1850), is a good example of a cast iron gents' urinal, several of which survive in the city.

BM28 CAMP HILL LOCKS
off Sandy lane, Bordesley
SP 085864 to 086857 ❑
The Warwick & Birmingham Canal falls through six locks on a course under railway viaducts (and recently diverted for a new road) to Bordesley Junction, whence a branch opened to Salford Junction in 1844) and to join the Birmingham Canal's Digbeth branch at Warwick Bar (B25).

BM29 THE BRASSHOUSE
Broad Street
SP 062867 **LSII** ❑
Brass was first produced in Birmingham in 1740, but the Birmingham New Brass and Spelter Company of 1781 was established expressly to counter the high price of Bristol brass. The works were demolished in 1866, the office building becoming the offices of the Birmingham Water Company. Now a restaurant.

BM30 GAS STREET BASIN
off Broad Street
SP 063866 ❑
The Birmingham Canal of 1769 and the first part of the Worcester & Birmingham Canal of 1795 were divided by a narrow strip of land, the Worcester Bar, over which goods were transhipped. A stop lock was made through the bar in 1815. The bar and lock survive, the latter crossed by a new cast iron roving bridge of traditional design. New build 'dockland' developments look across to a row of old cottages (**LSII**) on the west side.

BM30 Gas Street Basin

BM31 AQUEDUCT
Holliday Street
SP 064864 **LSII** ❑
The Worcester and Birmingham Canal and its wharves are carried over Holliday Street on cast columns and composite joists with brick-jack-arches, built 1880 by Handyside of Derby. The outer faces are of cast iron, decorated and brightly painted.

BM32 BOULTON & WATT MEMORIAL
Broad Street
SP 064868 ❑
James Watt, Matthew Boulton and William Murdoch are commemorated in bronze as they avidly discuss engine plans, by William Bloyes, erected 1956.

BM33 TOWN HALL
Victoria Square
SP 066869 **LSI** ❑
A competition for the design was won by J A Hansom, of Hansom cab fame, who was bankrupted by the financial failure of the builders. Opened 1834 but not completed until 1849, the building is a Corinthian temple outside and contains a fine concert hall which saw the first performances of Mendelssohn's *Elijah* and Elgar's *Dream of Gerontius*.

BM34 TRAM LINES
Edmund Street
SP 066871 ❑
This short length is the sole visible surviving example of Birmingham's extensive 3'6" electric street tramways, which operated from 1904 to 1953. This terminus went out of use in 1947.

BM35 COLLEGE OF ARTS AND CRAFTS
Margaret Street
SP 066870 **LSI** ✻
A fine example of municipal architecture, built 1881-5 by Martin & Chamberlain in brick and terracotta with encaustic tile friezes. A variety of building styles and materials can be seen in this part of the city.

BM36 MIDLAND BANK
Waterloo Street/Bennett's Hill
SP 068879 **LSII** ❑
Formerly the Birmingham Banking Company, the first joint stock bank established in the city. Designed by Thomas Rickman in Corinthian style and built 1831-2.

BM37 TELEPHONE EXCHANGE (former)
19 Newhall Street
SP 066874 **LSI** ✻
Birmingham's first exchange, designed 1896 by William Martin for the National Telephone Co. Brick and terracotta from J C Edwards, Ruabon, with lions' heads and attentive faces listening for the ringing of long silent telephones.

BM38 GREAT WESTERN ARCADE
Colmore Row
SP 071872 **LSII** ❑
Formerly a railway cutting approaching the GWR's Snow Hill station, the site was roofed over in 1874. The arcade, opened 1876 and renovated in 1976, closely follows the line of the tunnel. The re-faced north end does it no favours!

BM37 Birmingham's first telephone exchange

BM43 Guillotine lock at King Norton

BM39 LIBRARY & BATHS
Moseley Road, Balsall Heath
SP 080844 **LSII** ❑
Another fine example of civic pride expressed in brick and terracotta. The library dates from 1895 and the baths, with separate entrances for first class men, second class men, and classless women, were added in 1906/7. Both display the city's coat of arms, the library in terracotta and the baths in brightly painted plasterwork.

BM40 BIRMINGHAM RAILWAY MUSEUM
Warwick Road, Tyseley
SP 106841 ❑
A museum of locomotives, rolling stock and railway ephemera housed in the former GWR motive power depot. There is a programme of steam operating days (admission charge).

BM41 SAREHOLE MILL
Cole Bank Road, Hall Green
SP 099818 **LSII** ❑
A mill site since at least the C16th, it was leased by Matthew Boulton in 1756, probably for metal rolling. The present buildings date from the 1760s, and the two sets of corn milling gear from c.1850. The south wheel also powered a blade-grinding mill. Now a branch of the City's Museums, with milling, dairy and agricultural displays.

BM42 GARDEN SUBURB
off Linden Road, Bourneville
SP 044813 **LSII** ❑ ✻
Richard and George Cadbury built a new works and planned community here after 1879. The central open space was laid out in 1914, and the Junior School has a carillon tower. To the west are workers' cottages in differently arranged groups. In Bourneville Lane (SP 048810) there are two half-timbered factory lodges of c.1900 and various community buildings including baths of 1904; in Mary Vale Road (SP 036807) a fine quadrangle of almshouses, 1897.

BM43 STOP LOCK
off Broad Meadow Lane, Kings Norton
SP 056795 **LSII** ❑
The Stratford Canal (North section) of 1816 joins the Worcester and Birmingham (completed here 1796) via a stop lock with counter-weighted guillotine gates operated by hand winches. At the nearby junction there is a fine 2-storey canal cottage.

BM44 THE PATRICK COLLECTION
Lifford Lane, Kings Norton
SP 055796 ❑
Autoworld, a privately-owned motor museum featuring a private collection of period and dream cars. The old buildings, striped brick with red stretchers and blue headers, survive from a former mill (admission charge).

BM45 ROVER, LONGBRIDGE WORKS
Bristol Road South
SP 008776 ✻
Car manufacturing began here in 1905 when Herbert Austin left the Wolseley Sheep Shearing Machine Company in Aston, taking over a disused works which had made and colour-printed tin containers. In 1914 1,500 cars were produced, in 1926 25,000, and in 1950 165,700. An enormous works, the best building being a two-storey office on Bristol Road (west side). Crankshafts were forged by large steam hammers (Cincinatti) until 1988.

BM32 Memorial to Boulton, Watt and Murdoch

BIBLIOGRAPHY

Allen, G C — *The Industrial Development of Birmingham and the Black Country, 1860-1927*. George Allen & Unwin, 1929.

Barnsby, George J — *Social Conditions in the Black Country*, Integrated Publishing Services, 1980.

Barnsby, George J — *Birmingham Working People*. Integrated Publishing Services, 1989.

Brook, F — *Guide to the IA of the West Midlands*. Batsford, 1977.

Burritt, E — *Walks in the Black Country and its Green Borderland*. Sampson Low, 1868.

Court, W H B — *The Rise of Midland Industries, 1600-1838* OUP, 1938.

Cristiansen, Rex — *Regional History of the Railways of Great Britain* Vol 10; The West Midlands. David & Charles.

Greenslade, M V & Jenkins, J G (ed) — *Victoria County History of Stafford*, Vol 2. OUP, 1967.

Griffiths, Samuel — *Griffiths Guide to the Iron Trade of Great Britain* 1873 Reprinted by David & Charles, 1967.

Hackwood, F W — *Oldbury and round about*. Whitehead Bros, Wolverhampton, 1915.

Hadfield, Charles — *The Canals of the West Midlands*. David & Charles, 1966.

Hopkins, Eric — *Birmingham: the First Manufacturing Town in the World*. Weidenfeld & Nicholson, 1989.

Langford, J I — *The Staffordshire and Worcestershire Canal*. Goose & Son, 1974.

Lones, T E — *A History of Mining in the Black Country*. Herald Press, Dudley, 1898.

Parsons, Harold — *Portrait of the Black Country*. Robert Hale, 1986.

Raven, Jon — *The Urban and Industrial Songs of the Black Country and Birmingham*. Broadside, Wolverhampton, 1977.

Raybould, Trevor J — *The Economic Emergence of the Black Country*. David & Charles, 1973.

Rowlands, Marle B — *The West Midlands from AD1800*. Longman UK, 1987.

Timmins, Samuel (ed) — *Birmingham and the Midland Hardware District* (Reports by the Local Industries Committee of the British Association in Birmingham, in 1865). Robert Hardwicke, 1866.

West Midlands Group — *Conurbation*. The Architectural Press, 1948.

Williams, N — *Black Country Folk at Werk*. Uralia Press, 1989.

Blowers Green, Dudley, c.1885, showing the canal lock with derelict furnaces, mine pumping engines—and subsidence—all part of a classic Black Country scene